JERICHO UNMASKED

An Entrapped Lesbian's
Journey to Freedom

CARI GINTZ

JERICHO UNMASKED

An Entrapped Lesbian's Journey to Freedom

CARI GINTZ

REDEMPTION PRESS

Published by Redemption Press, PO Box 427, Enumclaw, WA 98022

Toll Free (844) 2REDEEM (273-3336)

Redemption Press is honored to present this title in partnership with the author. The views expressed or implied in this work are those of the author. Redemption Press provides our imprint seal representing design excellence, creative content, and high quality production.

Scripture quotations taken from the New American Standard Bible® (NASB) Copyright © 1960, 1962, 1963, 1968, 1971, 1972, 1973, 1975, 1977, 1995 by The Lockman Foundation. Used by permission. www.Lockman.org

All names have been changed unless prior approval was received

ISBN: 978-1-68314-656-8
       978-1-68314-657-5 (ePub)
       978-1-68314-658-2 (Mobi)

Cover design by One Red Phoenix

Library of Congress Catalog Card Number: 2018947698

Endorsements

Cari Gintz divulges the abuse and trauma she experienced as a child. I admire her honesty and openness. She also shows how children can be set up to fall into a trap created by the Enemy of our souls. I believe this book will bring liberation to others who have felt they needed to remain silent about what they endured as a child and the outcome of the sins committed against them.

—Denise Shick
Author of *My Daddy's Secret* and founder of Help 4 Families

Cari's story greatly increased my understanding of a struggle that many face, and *Jericho Unmasked* will enlighten those looking for real hope and deep understanding. Her faith-building, transforming journey displays God's power and great love, which will encourage and bring hope and joy to the reader.

—Dale Piscura
Pastor of Men's Discipleship, Cuyahoga Valley Church,
Broadview Heights, Ohio

We walked alongside of Cari Gintz during the 2014 Gay Games in Cleveland. I could see she has a great heart for people, though to be honest, I didn't quite "get" her. Having tackled this must-read autobiography, we now praise God for her love for Jesus, her determination to walk bravely, the prayers of her mother, and the deep respect and burden for all the ones her life's path has touched. Be challenged, be encouraged, and be blessed by God's story in and through her.

—Pastor Joe and Debbie Abraham
Scranton Road Bible Church, Cleveland, Ohio

Acknowledgments

Deep thanks to my informal editing team for taking the time to review proof copies (sometimes multiple times): Leah, Rosalie, Kathy, Julia. Many thanks to Catherine for collaboration on the title and to all the family and friends who have partnered in prayer. I love and appreciate all of you.

To Dori, the Editorial Manager of Redemption Press: It requires a unique talent to retain an author's voice, edit the language to maintain intent, and guide a new author in a collaborative way. You, my dear friend, mastered all of it. The guidance, deliberation, and most of all the prayerful consideration of every word was a blessing delivered directly from the Father. I am grateful this is not the end of the story. You are my friend for life!

This book is dedicated to my dear daughter. We have come a long way in our journey. So blessed and honored that God gave me you!

Table of Contents

Foreword

Jericho Unmasked is a tribute to the kindness of God to capture a beautiful, one-of-a-kind passionate soul, Cari Gintz, for the glory of God! The Church cannot have enough stories of the incredible grace of God reaching down and transforming a soul. Her book is about the redeeming power of grace and the kindness of God in Jesus Christ our Lord to reach down and unravel many years of pain, trauma, and distorted thinking as a lesbian. God has touched Cari's soul and revealed she has always been the "apple of His eye" and that Cari is His gem who has always belonged to Him, even when she strayed.

This is a story about how God wooed Cari back to Himself in all the twists and turns of her painful life in homosexuality. It's about restoration and redemption! Cari continues her courageous process of being transparent before the Lord and people! She demonstrates a path of continued yielding and allowing God to use her life, and thus bring hope in the power of prayer. She is an example of releasing the reins of her life, trusting and waiting upon Him. Cari inspires the reader to believe God in making a difference in loved ones. Be inspired by Cari to believe and to have hope in God to change your loved ones, even if it takes years! Cari's story shows us that God is always near to those who seek Him, as He is the One who began this relationship with us, and He is the One who finishes it!

Stephen H. Black, Executive Director, First Stone Ministries
Author of *Freedom Realized and Freedom Realized—The Complete First Stone Ministries Effectiveness Survey Report*
Oklahoma City, Oklahoma
www.stephenblack.org

Introduction

I lived the majority of my life inside the walls of the bustling city of Los Angeles, California. Within those walls, the sun shone bright most of the time. However, my own self-contained, walled-in fortress of brokenness stood high and was the greatest blockage to realizing God's purpose for my life. For a number of years, I lived in the shadows, those places shaded most of the day because the "wall" blocked the sun. Occasionally I would welcome the light, but I hid in the dark, seemingly free from conviction, and lived life on my terms.

I was physically and psychologically entrapped and spiritually depraved. The walls were so high and strong that no human could get in or out.

One day a miracle of sudden freedom occurred for this undeserving woman whom God saw before the foundation of the world. I suspect that many, given the opportunity, would have eagerly composed the next chapters of my life, and I doubt that they would have been positive and uplifting chronicles. Instead they might have reflected the continued downward trajectory into the pit of hell, which, based on my state, would have been the logical conclusion. Yet God saw me before I was even a formed substance in my mother's womb. I'm grateful that the chapters He penned for my life are filled with redemption, hope, transformation, and eternity with Him.

I have often pondered why I am not cynical, hard, or simply disgusted with God. We are all fearfully and wonderfully made, and I firmly believe the Lord wired me in such a manner that vulnerability and childlike wonder will always take precedence even in the midst of tragedy, pain, and deep hurts. I do not consider this attitude my own doing or casually chalk it up to well-developed survival techniques. I give all the credit to God and am deeply thankful. In His amazing grace, He also constructed me as relational, outgoing, and flexible to the degree that living peaceably without regrets, forgiving above being right, and resolving to preserve relationships are tenets I hold dear to my heart. My hope is that these relational imperatives ring loudly throughout my story. I refuse to expose or demean anyone or capitalize on injury and pain. Instead, I choose to display God's relentless work of redemption and continued transformation.

Nothing in my life is random or arbitrary. A divine scarlet cord is woven throughout my story as a constant reminder of the exquisite hand of God in the context of the whole. Would I alter a single day in my life? No. Would I want to relive all the chapters? No, especially the dark and painful ones. Yet to live in regret is failure to embrace the present. He has equipped me to share all that has been written on my heart—an epistle to be read and known by all. If a single day had changed, every subsequent day would have been altered. If I truly embrace the biblical truth in Psalm 139:16—"Thine eyes have seen my unformed substance and, in Thy book, they were all written, the days that were ordained for me, when as yet there was not one of them"—then regret cannot be a part of my present and future hope.

As I tell my story, I've inserted poems that underscore my experience, but the actual date of composition was not necessarily commensurate with the exact life stage.

In 2003, years before the Lord seized my heart and set me free from a life that cut me to pieces, I woke up in the middle of the night. I had written a few poems over the years, but this one was different, as it was far from my life's truth at the time. I believe the Lord scribed "Purpose" through my hands with a view to the reality I would one day embrace. Since the day I penned it, many of its lines have been brought to my mind in certain circumstances, and I have had to pause and listen to the Lord's reminder. This composition is just a simple example of a God who saw the whole landscape of my life and all He destined for me.

Purpose

Where did all the years go as life comes to a close?

Are the snapshots plain to see, or are they unexposed?

Did I grip the bitter moments as trophies all my own?

Or melt their grandeur down and distribute polished stones?

Did I take the harsh, cold winters and with spring remain inside?

Or appreciate each season and choose there to abide?

Did I stand so tall that others could not see within my eyes?

Or kneel level with their hearts and hear the inner cries?

Did I fan the flames of fiery rage over justifying the truth?

Or let morning dew reduce to ash knowing character needs no proof?

Did I comfort in my prisons, hanging pictures on the walls?

Or allow Him to unlock and walk down freedom's halls?

Did I crumble under rocks of pride with injuries prolonged?

Or let those wiser dig me out, admitting I wasn't strong?

Did I shake my fists at heaven, demanding answers why?

Or recognize more wisdom represents the best reply?

Did I take each chapter written, seal it for my selfish prize?

Or generate an epilogue to share with younger lives?

Did moments pass in emptiness with conflicts in the soul?

Or were the last words on my lips, "I truly do feel whole"?

Considering this poem, my heart is to be transparent with exposed snapshots but cautious so that intrigue does not overshadow God's mighty hand. "Gay" and "homosexuality" are enticing subjects these days. So if you find yourself craving more details, I apologize in advance and hope the Lord will simply reveal His main purpose of the book and His thoughts toward you while you are progressing through the pages.

The closing Bible passage before launching into my story is Jeremiah 15:18–19. The Lord gave me these verses after a large loss in my life, but I did not know at the time how He would use them in my future:

> Why has my pain been perpetual
> And my wound incurable, refusing to be healed?
> Will You indeed be to me a deceptive stream
> With water that is unreliable?
> Therefore, thus says the Lord,
> "If you return, then I will restore you—
> Before Me you will stand;
> And if you extract the precious from the worthless,
> You will become My spokesman."

Lord, let it be so as I press on to write.

Chapter 1

Family Dynamics and Shattering

I was the firstborn and "cute as a button," according to my mom and my grandma, when I popped into this world on May 29, 1957, in the heart of Southern California, but my core was fallen because of sin. I will pose the age-old question right off the bat—born gay? I find this to be curious and want to clarify that for me, the point is moot. The package was God's perfect design. The insides contained a soul that, left to its own devices, would willingly and deliberately defy God. "Behold, I was brought forth in iniquity, and in sin my mother conceived me" (Psalm 51:5). So when I am asked about being born gay, I cannot answer for certain. What I do know is that born gay or not born gay does not give license to live a life that is in complete rebellion to God's relational design and purpose for our lives as prescribed in the Bible. Even if a stand against the contrary cultural tide results in persecution, rejections, or loss of relationships, I must first honor God.

From the time I was born, Satan and all of the powers of hell had a keen eye on me. The mouths of hell are hungry for humans, to either stop their births entirely or make sure they live their lives separated from God. When I came into this world, I had a multitude of chinks in my fleshly armor. Satan, being the father of lies and the embodiment of darkness, knew exactly how to capitalize on those chinks and how to structure environmental circumstances that would ultimately lead to choices, *my* choices. All these wrong choices would result in spiritual, psychological, and physical damage at the deepest level. Satan is not bigger than God. I also know that God is sovereign and sees the entire landscape and nothing will thwart His hand. However, our choices matter. My life provides a little glimpse into the bigness of God. He had a tether on me from a young age and was fully in charge every step of the way. My God never had to revert to a plan B.

My grandmother on my father's side was an enigma. Ninety pounds and nicknamed "Cricket," she laughed about things that others would consider disturbing. Her loss of babies in the womb due to an abusive husband was conveyed in the same manner as a discussion about the weather forecast. She never showed facial expressions exhibiting pain, anger, or hurt in spite of horrors in her past.

A grandmother might have a favorite grandchild, though she would maintain some level of protocol so as not to hurt her favorite's siblings. But mine was the opposite. She was open and matter of fact that my younger sister was less than second best. In my grandmother's eyes, the sun rose and set on my head, and I was "the light of her life." My strong resemblance to her contributed to this—a petite frame, long dark hair, and greenish-brown eyes.

Going to Grandma's house was a treat, especially after the arrival of my sister three and a half years after my birth. Grandma's place was an environment without borders. The house appeared significantly larger than my home, with high ceilings, and I loved the expanse. Also, I did not have to compete for affection.

My mother always said I was an easy baby and lovable. I enjoyed cuddling and being in close proximity to my mom. But when the foreign intruder entered (my sister, Katie), I pulled away. The shift in my behavior from clingy to distant compelled my mother to seek advice from her pediatrician. The doctor convinced her that I would "come back." Unfortunately, psychology had not matured to the degree it has today. That advice did not pan out, and I never really "returned." In fact, I shut down and traveled inward to a safe little bubble where I did not feel rejected. Vocalization of wants turned to silent cries.

At the young age of five, I pondered meaning as I glanced at the immense blue sky and embraced my smallness. I simply watched life and recorded it, yet I had no capacity to appropriately interpret or even express my pain. So trips to Grandma's house represented full-time attention. I did not have to speak. Grandma did all the talking and ministered to my every need, as perceived through the heart of a young child.

A typical day as a five-year-old at Grandma's was coffee in the morning, followed by peanut butter and white-sugar sandwiches while watching afternoon soap operas. *As the World Turns* especially captured my interest.

My grandma told me stories of the abuse my father received under the hands of her ex-husband, my biological grandfather. She laughed hysterically when recounting how my dad had been tied to a tree for twenty-four hours, almost freezing to death.

My dad was a track star in high school, and he gained his best training while running from his own father. Fortunately, my father was one of the babies who survived the trauma in her womb, or I would not be alive today. Unfortunately, she had desired a daughter and clothed my dad in dresses until he entered school. I received my own private slide show of the young boy in lace. These stories unfolded in a continuous mantra until I was nine, as if I might forget some pertinent detail.

The dentist was later able to correct the nine cavities that resulted from trips to Grandma's house. But no human physician could cure the visual, verbal, and physical imprints on my mind, heart, body, and soul.

I never met my biological grandfather. Instead, Uncle Max, the renter who lived at my grandmother's house after World War II, became my surrogate grandfather. They were not married, and it was purely friendship. Evenings were spent on Uncle Max's lap in a large overstuffed chair with my very own pint-size flannel shirt, a geeky pocket pencil holder, and a miniature corncob pipe. My grandmother usually sat on the couch, quite far away.

I wanted to be just like Uncle Max, yet I did not realize until years later that he'd awakened what God designed to be pure and fresh within marriage. As we watched *Laurel and Hardy* and *The Three Stooges*, I was anesthetized by belly laughter and the warm embrace. What I could not process was the differentiation of hands that subtly moved like delicate surgical instruments away from appropriate places of safety to cuddle unauthorized areas of my underdeveloped body.

I am not certain if my grandmother ever knew about the sexual abuse. I returned to that house as an adult, and the distance in the living room between the overstuffed chair and the couch my grandmother occupied was shockingly small, even though the furniture still resided in the same spots. I sometimes wonder if subconsciously I gave her an excuse for failing to protect me, by imagining a much-longer room with expansive distance, as if my grandmother was too far away to rescue me.

Uncle Max was used greatly by the Enemy to shatter the mind of a young girl, warp all sense of identity, and encase me in a lonely world filled with shame. This violation had an undeniable impact in the many years to come.

My father was a man of many words for many people, but he had few words for his own family. By all rights my father should have been cynical and hard because of his upbringing. Ironically, he was the opposite. He had a simplistic vulnerability. He recognized the beauty in things that many would just perceive as being in the way. If a child screamed in a store, he smiled with the empathy of watching an adorable kid. When traversing a stream, he didn't simply stumble over rocks to get from one place to the next—he noticed the beauty of the rocks as a necessary and integral part of his journey.

He never looked back, discussed his childhood, or revealed his quiet pain and heartache. On the contrary, he embraced and savored each morsel of life. He had an interest in and love of all kinds of people, and he had an amazing ability to "read" an individual. Within a few short minutes, he could probe a person, leave the scene, and know their whole life. He displayed little of himself, as he never wanted to burden anyone. Through wisdom and insight, he knew that life was too short to dwell on anything less than magic, wonder, and most of all, hope.

A voracious reader, he would describe places in the world, and one would think he had been there. His imagination and boyish curiosity allowed him to travel to places in his mind time and time again, and in those travels he had many safe places—different from his formative years. My father had no problem crying, and he never apologized for it. A memorable Christmas day was when he described the movie *Life Is Beautiful*. He could barely get the words out, but his eyes revealed passion and the tears that flowed as he relived that father's protection over his son. That day I saw a compelling depth in my father and an unmatched sensitivity.

Fabulous at cards, my father played contract bridge—a highly skilled level of cards involving tactics, communication, memory, and probability. Although quite serious about the game among his buddies for many years, he knew what was important in life. Soon after his mother had passed, we played a family poker game that turned heated. My dad was the best at the table, and everyone else had lost sight of the plot. It was not about winning. For my father, the important piece was the relational aspect of playing together. So when the harsh superlatives flew, he folded his cards, put his head on the table, cried, and said, "I just lost my mother, and you all do not know how fortunate you are to have each other as brothers, and you fight."

That was another moment when time stopped and I paused to ponder.

My father often took me deep-sea fishing, and once when the waves were high, I was horribly woozy. My dad just kept on fishing with joy. Rock cod was the catch of the day, and his line bent with six of them at a time. My utter seasickness diminished my amazement. I finally lay on the deck, inhaling the fumes of the burgers cooking in the galley, and just wanted to know, *When are we going home?* That long sea trip taught me how to be rugged. Those waves could have been twenty feet, and my dad would not have left those fish!

My dad never judged. He had a sense of humor that one might perceive as judgmental, but it was not. He simply watched people and sometimes made private comments that others wished they could get away with. He'd laugh, and no one was worse for the wear. People gave him the grace to be himself because he extended the same.

He didn't have long, in-depth conversations about life, no heavy discussions about the state of the world, and definitely no sharing of hurts and pains. But the treasures in life are not always the obvious ones. Sometimes, and more importantly, it's the connection of the heart combined with the security in knowing that love, resolve, forgiveness, vulnerability, fearless abandonment to live life to its fullest, and hope are what lasts. My father imparted these silent legacies to me, and they still remain to this day.

As a child, I did not know he struggled with homosexuality. It was a shock years later to find this out through a long-held secret shared by my sister. Although my father had served in World War II, his mission was "casual engagement" with others to secure information rather than actual battle. The love of his life was a young man serving on the front lines, who was tragically killed. I cannot fathom what my father went through in the 1940s to retain such a deep secret and incredible loss. I imagine he buried it in the same coffin his lover occupied.

I did not approach my father and ask questions or dig deep when this discovery came to light. Sometimes survival mechanisms are not meant to be arbitrarily tampered with by ignorant humans attempting to crack the lid to get information or deep answers. God will reveal it in His gentle time. If He doesn't, then it remains as part of the mystery of His sovereignty. If this fact of my father's had been probed prematurely, all the stamina and vigor he had left could have been killed, and even his heart, which had beaten strong for eighty years, could have been stopped. The added knowledge explained a tremendous amount in relation to the family dynamics and the strained relationship of my parents. My father did the best he could with the capacity he had.

I know wholeheartedly I will see my father in heaven. His relationship with Christ was not readily visible, but if the eyes are the window to the soul, there is where the relationship could be seen. I believe he cried many quiet tears, and I will ask him when I see him again if I can take a tour of *his* bottles of tears too. God personally labels them all, and amazing grace is the epilogue of bottled moments.

My mother had dealt with her own identity issues during her youth. She was predominantly raised by her father, and he had wanted a boy, so he cut my mom's hair short. Up until the time of puberty, she'd wondered if she was in fact a boy.

My grandmother was diagnosed with multiple sclerosis when my mom was five. Her dad decided he would get his daughter a new-and-improved mommy, and he abandoned his wife. The new-and-improved mommy, concerned about her image as a stepmother, later insisted upon charm school for her stepdaughter.

My mother was brilliant and years ahead of her classmates. She graduated with the highest honors from Rice University at nineteen, obtaining an accounting degree. But because of this acceleration, the social aspects of growing up did not have an opportunity to develop. The majority of her classmates were three years older and had interests far different from my mother's. Unable to relate to them on any emotional or psychological level, she was excluded from social engagements simply for being too young. However, her ability with numbers was unmatched, and her sharp mind was the only way she was equal to her older classmates.

In her early twenties, Mom fell madly in love with a World War II fighter pilot. He was shot down and went undiscovered for five long years. My mother had moved to the West Coast to be closer to the port of his return. His death shattered her when she finally heard the news.

In the early 1950s, single women approaching thirty were under considerable pressure to marry. My father was extremely handsome and much better at dating than being a husband. After six months of weekend dating, Mom agreed to marry him.

Shortly after I was born, my mother had a deep encounter with Christ. She recognized she was capable of any sin under the sun but by the grace of God was redeemed from a destiny of rebellion. She submitted herself to the transforming work of Christ from the day she received Him, but it was not without struggle and hardship.

Women need to be loved, and my father did not have the ability to embrace and experience intimacy with a wife. Although Dad exhibited amazing qualities, he had dissociative disorder—a disconnection between thoughts, identity, and consciousness—likely due to his childhood abuse, and he was incapable of deep connection with those closest to him. His unaddressed struggle with homosexuality also had undeniable consequences in their relationship, and tension and bitterness filled our home. To add to the distress and anxiety was my dad's knowledge that his wife had deeply loved another man, although his angst was never directly addressed.

But my mom persevered in her marriage based on her strong commitment to the Lord and her children's welfare. She made sure her children knew they were loved.

Mom believed in vitamins and a daily helping of Gerber's liver baby food to keep the body strong. Every morning for breakfast,

I ate healthy cereal followed by the half jar of the baby food and a handful of supplements. I grew to like it, and as a result, I never missed a day of school from kindergarten to sixth grade with the exception of normal childhood maladies, such as the chicken pox.

My mother led a disciplined and organized life. A bookkeeper by trade, she could readily convey how much she had spent on groceries the first week of June 1989. When I was ten, she offered me a sizable monthly allowance of forty dollars. This was 1967, so forty dollars went a long way. But there was a catch. With this allowance, I had to buy everything, including school clothes, beyond the necessities. If I wanted to buy a school lunch, it came out of my money.

When go-go boots were the fad, I sat in the shoe store for a full hour pondering whether these boots were worth it. Finally, I looked up at the shoe salesman and said, "I am really sorry. I cannot afford them."

The man looked at my mother in astonishment. To this day, there are no clothes in my closet that sit idle, and no purchase is void of a thought process.

Most importantly, she instilled in me the principle of tithing. Each month I took four dollars off the top and put it in my tithe envelope. Occasionally, I mowed lawns for the neighbors or babysat their young children. If I earned a dollar, ten cents went into the envelope for church. This habit of tithing has never departed, even during my depth of darkness, and I thank my mother for instilling this at such a young age. My mother taught me discipline and to never put off the hard stuff. Do it first and get it over with. She was the opposite of procrastinator, and I value these lessons to this day.

None of us is given a little handbook for mothers, so when I came on the scene, my mom had no real example. A mother who was sick, followed by a stepmother only interested in outward development, were not solid foundations. In spite of the hardships and family struggles, I know my mother loved me with her whole heart and always held me with open hands. She wholeheartedly recognized from the time I was born that I ultimately belonged to the Lord. I was not her possession but simply a gift delivered to her care. She knew her main job as a parent was to point me to Christ.

Chapter 2

The Incorruptible Seed of Salvation

When in kindergarten, I was extremely disruptive. I also started to feverishly bite my nails, a habit I did not stop until my early fifties. Perhaps on some level I was crying out to be seen. My sister had seemingly taken over, certainly through no fault of her own. She was a normal baby with needs, and she expressed those needs. I afforded her the forefront as I retreated to the shadows with the hidden secret of abuse embedded and further nourished during visits to Grandma's, contributing to my behavioral issues.

Notes were sent home daily from my kindergarten teacher, but I could not change. No matter how hard I tried to be nice, it was impossible. I looked for every opportunity to create havoc, and I was smart enough to find ways to do it. I convinced some less savvy children that some dirt in the playground tasted good, but they cried when the aftereffect was less than favorable. I adopted an innocent face, but inside I laughed hysterically.

Sometimes I went into the coat closet and moved jackets and sweatshirts, and kids would get distressed because they could not find their garments. I squirmed and made others giggle at nap time. I could not grasp why anyone had to sleep during the day.

On numerous occasions though, in my quiet space, I looked up at the sky and wondered what was there and where I fit.

One night when I was five and a half years old, I lay in my bed, crying and distraught. I told my mom, "I just cannot be better."

My mother sat next to my bed and shared Jesus with me. "Honey, you cannot change. It is impossible. The only way you can change is to receive Jesus in your heart. His life is the only thing that will change you, because He will come in and change you from the inside. You can't just decide to change."

As giant tears streamed down my face, I cried, and that night I received Jesus in my heart. I told Him I was sorry for all my sins. I had a slew to recall, even in my short life. I knew at that moment something had transpired.

The next day was normal. I was not aware of my changed life. I just skipped into class. At the end of the day, the teacher handed me an envelope with a sealed note inside. I was frightened, as I had received these notes before. I scanned the day in my mind and wondered what I had done wrong. Usually I knew. This note was far different though. The teacher was puzzled: *What happened to Cari?* Even at the age of five and a half, God had started His transformational work in my life. He is "the author and perfecter of faith" (Hebrews 12:2).

As a child I attended multiple churches of every denomination: Baptist, Pentecostal, Nazarene, Presbyterian. (While attending the Presbyterian church in Bel Air, I even shook Ronald Reagan's hand when he was a movie star in Westerns.) I attended Sunday school, heard the Word, and performed my due diligence to memorize the books of the Bible and key verses. I received many pins and gold stars.

School, on the other hand, was a mixed bag. Studying and achieving perfect grades became my sole purpose. I was driven and disciplined. If homework was due in three weeks, I finished it in two. The stress of the "incomplete" made me crazy. I attribute much of this discipline to my mother, the epitome of organized. Yet even with all of the effort, I was not the prettiest or the smartest. There was always that girl who edged out in front, who was noticed, who was the teacher's pet. I felt odd, because the things I contemplated were a little too deep for the average eight- to twelve-year-old. I thought about meaning and purpose and was keenly aware that I had terrible fingernails and everyone else had beautiful hands. I wanted love and friendship and deep connection. I was surrounded by a crowd but lonely inside with my thoughts about God, the world, and why.

Kids were cruel. In the fifth grade I was fond of a popular boy. I thought he was funny, and other girls had "boys." I entrusted my closest friends with this information. One day on the playground, this boy approached me and asked me to come behind the building in private to talk. He proceeded to ask me to go steady and gave me a little bubblegum ring. I was excited and in disbelief, only to find out that a crowd of girls, including my trusted friends, were observing us. I realized it was all a big joke. Words fall short in conveying what occurred inside that day. Betrayal, shame, and heartbreak were key hallmarks of the emotion, but worse, a deeper shattering feeling that I was not worthy.

A few days later I was in class preparing for an exam. The fifth-grade teacher was cruel. He had balding red hair and a temper that would make even an adult shudder. I was always nervous when taking a test under the compulsion to be perfect, so I would grip my pencil and bite my nails. This teacher came up behind me and in front of the class said, "How hard are you going to grip that pencil and chew your fingers?" He proceeded to laugh, and then the whole class laughed. I traveled to a place in my mind where no one else was allowed. I finished the test and received high marks. I survived, but barely.

I didn't share these events with my parents. What for? It was probably my own fault. I was unable to control my world, but I could control my grades. Sometimes I just cried in my bed, and Jesus would gently stroke my face and wipe the tears.

I started piano lessons when I was six, with a very strict female teacher. Although I practiced only ten minutes per day, I excelled in recitals until I was eleven years old. One day the piano teacher yelled and screamed and rapped my knuckles. She scared me, and I told my mom I wanted to quit. I never said why, simply using the excuse that I wanted to play outside.

A couple of years later, I attended a school concert and was hypnotized by the harmonious and heartfelt sounds the new piano teacher at school created as he played his own composition. His face was kind, and I wanted to play just like him.

My parents sacrificed to give me lessons, and for three years I adored going to his home and watching the keys dance under my fingers. That was such a positive influence because he listened and allowed me to play a mix of compositions I enjoyed. He complimented my efforts while providing guidance and direction. Most of all, he smiled. Unfortunately, my parents did not have a lot of money, and lessons became too expensive.

Summer camp was a big part of my church experience. I loved camp and held the female counselors in awe. I wanted to be close to them and even strove to be their favorite by behaving perfectly and doing all the chores when asked. The craving for attention and love moved front and center.

I enjoyed sleepovers and spending time with friends. The boys were OK, but the girls were the best. Perhaps every pubescent child goes through this desire for attention, but my need was extreme. Sometimes I wished that something horrible would happen, just to experience attention. Although my home life was good, I experienced little affection or touch, and by age twelve, I did not need it—so I thought. My parents did the best they could with the tools they had and the good advice they received. (God's handprints are on every aspect of my life, so my intention is never to place blame or fault.)

Up to age thirteen, engagement with the opposite sex was more like puppy love. In the mid to late 1960s, television was under censorship scrutiny. There was no internet or social media, and preteen children were still young and innocent for the most part. In elementary school there were the occasional spin the bottle games that resulted in far more giggling than actual physical contact with the opposite sex. This was fortunate, as I was very conscious of my uneasiness with the boys and the inner tension that these games invoked. However, I would not have been able to explain it.

I had a girlfriend who lived across the street with a raving alcoholic father. She and I experimented a bit sexually. I felt extremely guilty though. (I know this is not an abnormal event during puberty, so I am not assigning heavy weight to it.) The irony was that I was not paralyzed by the physical engagement and felt quite at ease with her. At that time, the Uncle Max encounters still occurred as I went on a number of vacations alone with him and Grandma until I was fourteen.

Junior high, though, launched me into a different scene. I faced extreme pressure to go beyond kissing, especially at parties. The games intensified, and the giggling ceased. My paralysis with the opposite sex manifested like an invasive cancer. It was hidden well, yet I knew I was completely trapped. I viewed boys more like a piece of art. Some were fine art, but I was more comfortable just admiring them. Sometimes I inched close enough, and they were able to take advantage of the paralysis. On most occasions I felt completely dead and separate from my own body. I had no voice, and I had no capacity to set boundaries—a toxic dilemma for a teenage girl. I could not ascertain why the word *no* seemed to rest in my throat. I had great dialogue in my own head and occasionally by myself out loud, yet in the presence of the opposite sex, silence shrouded my being.

High school was better, as I finally exited that awful gawky stage. Contacts replaced horn-rimmed glasses, my clothing style improved, and my skin turned brown as nutmeg in the summer, as I took after my Cherokee Indian dad. In sunny California, the tanner you were, the hotter you were. I spent my summers bathed in baby oil on Venice Beach for hours on end, and the result was that I got noticed. Brown and beautiful. It became another element so core to my identity that as I turned white in the winter, I would get depressed, and if I missed a day of tanning or the sun did not shine, I felt I had to sunbathe the minute the sun came out.

Dating was a struggle though. I wanted love. The boys wanted something else—no surprise, of course. The good "church boys" were no better. In addition to my extreme dilemma of having little to no boundaries, I had a wildly active conscience. But God's protection took center stage. I could have progressed into extreme amounts of trouble with long-term consequences. By God's tremendous grace, my conscience and the seed of God remained alive and well.

Broken relationships with guys and deep hurts of rejection continued through high school. I participated on the drill team, because I was not good enough or popular enough to be a cheerleader. That seemed to be the story of my life—just slightly behind and never able to catch up. In the midst of it all, I subtly noticed I was emotionally drawn to women. Terms like *gay, homosexual,* and *lesbian* were not spoken in society in the early seventies. The mere mention of such would have been construed as weird.

I did not take my attraction to a sexual extreme with *these* women. It manifested more in a desire to be close to them. I enjoyed my friends. But with the girl across the street, my secret pal, we grew braver in our experimentation until the death of her father and her family's departure from the neighborhood.

Ouija boards, séances, and curiosity about other worlds consumed many sleepovers with girlfriends. Given my early curiosity about life's meaning, this activity blended well with seeking what was beyond. Some moments were frightening, as they went far outside the realm of fun and games to scary and dark. On one occasion, the little Ouija board triangle moved by itself. If someone had told me this had happened, I would not have believed it. But I saw it, and it freaked me out.

Throughout these explorations, I was still going to summer church camps and had grown particularly fond of one of my camp counselors, who was twenty-one, which seemed old at the time, as I was in my midteens. She befriended me and invited me to dinner with her boyfriend. This relationship, combined with the dabbling in darkness, paved the way for an even deeper loneliness and emotional dismissal of my parents.

On one occasion back at home, I woke up in the middle of the night, made my bed, wrote a note to my mom, climbed out the window, hopped onto my bike, and rode to this counselor's house. To this day my mother still has that fated note, and I have asked God's forgiveness, as I know it jolted her deeply. My mother was smart enough to know where I had probably gone, as she keenly observed the attachment. Needless to say, the counselor defended me when my mom showed up at the counselor's home in the early hours of the morning the next day. She adamantly told my mom that my parents had no clue about parenting, and this deepened my draw to this woman. My mom loaded my bike into the trunk and drove me home. The quietness of that six-mile ride was deafening.

My dad had waited outside for us to arrive. That was the first time I'd seen my father cry. I stood on the front yard screaming while I watched the pain on my parents' faces. My identity was shattering piece by piece, and my insides were out of control.

Innocent as they might seem to some, those dark games were instruments of evil and anything but innocuous. They opened a door of darkness the Enemy would have loved to exploit. This evil open door was a key trigger that prompted me to run away. When that camp counselor got married, I was heartbroken but never showed anything other than a smile. At this juncture, with virtually no identity left and an inner depression that could not be conquered, I was ripe and ready for the next extreme chapter of my life—The Local Church, with a capital *T*.

Chapter 3

Vortex of The Local Church

In 1975, during my senior year in high school, my mother discovered that Witness Lee, the protégé of Chinese Christian martyr Watchman Nee, had set up a church in San Fernando Valley, not too far from our home. My mother had attended the Local Church (LC) in Los Angeles for a brief period about fifteen years earlier, shortly after I was born. The premise was based on One Church, One City, and the largest claim was that the LC was the Lord's recovery on the earth today. A key tenet was "to come out and be separate and touch not the unclean." This is a biblical call. But the LC took this to such an extreme that it made traditional Christianity seem like the liberal left wing.

Watchman Nee and his writings are extremely biblical and profound. When Witness Lee came to this country, his goal was to bring these writings to the foreground. Witness Lee firmly believed he was "God's man on the earth today" and the oracle of God—similar to Moses—and he expounded on the words of Watchman Nee.

The LC was an insular environment. If a believer was not attending the One Church, One City, they were deemed as excluded from the Lord's recovery and would not be one of the firstfruits at His return. One might even spend a thousand years in outer darkness as punishment for not embracing the Lord's recovery.

My mom and dad took my sister and me to our first service at the LC in the San Fernando Valley location. It was filled with people both young and old, though the lion's share of attendees were between seventeen and thirty years old. I was seventeen, and my sister was fourteen. I walked in with my dark tan and cute clothes and stood out. The guys (a.k.a. "brothers") wore either white, baby blue, or tan shirts with khaki pants, and the women (a.k.a "sisters") had on skirts below the knee, frumpy tops, doily-type lace head coverings, no makeup, no jewelry, and basic hairstyles. Men sat on one side of the room and women on the other. Since they all faced each other, the women had little towels that they placed over their legs.

Well, I sat there and thought, *Wow, I could be top of the heap in this strange place!* The people were gracious, giving us an over-abundance of attention. We were invited to meals as a family, and I embraced the camaraderie like a duck takes to water. We started attending each week, and I did not have to bring a little cloth because I wore cute pants. Those frumpy little outfits were out of the question.

I continued attending in my senior year, and the sisters would come over to meet with my mom and "pray-read" the Word, a practice where one reads the words and prays over them, repeating the words over and over. An "Oh Lord Jesus" mantra filled the house, and sometimes when I would appear, the "Oh Lord Jesus" would change its tone (to show disapproval of my clothing).

At the beginning of my senior year, while still seventeen, I secured an after-school job at Rubber Supply Co. It was just me and the owner at the site. He was a short man and extremely ugly, by anyone's standards. I learned about the business and became efficient at pulling product, packaging it, and developing shipping labels at record speed. I considered it a personal challenge to meet or exceed the previous day's output.

The company was in a large garage-type setting with a big door. We did not get customers, just shipments of supplies and pickups by carriers. Psychologically and emotionally stunted, I was unskilled at recognizing signs that this environment could lead to trouble.

One day my boss suddenly shut the big door and asked if we could take a break. He proceeded to convey his desire for a daughter and asked to sit behind me while we read a magazine. I knew in my heart what was about to occur, and I froze. What I thought were well-developed survival techniques turned on me that day, as fear paralyzed my body and my voice. He groped my immobile body. The screams inside never entered the atmosphere of that dark warehouse. The Enemy used this evil and wicked man to further the shattering of my soul.

I told no one, as I thought it was my fault. The next day I drove to work and asked for my paycheck. He tried to give me five extra dollars, and I wanted to vomit. I threw the five-dollar bill in his face and drove away without saying a word. I never went back, but I shook in my bed for weeks and held the secret tight to my heart. This was the perfect storm for the Enemy to perpetuate his mission of destruction. Soon I shut it down in my mind, tucking it away in the place that the other tragedies had been stored. The space was getting crowded, as Uncle Max consumed considerable real estate.

School wasn't any sort of refuge. Although I had friends, at my core I felt out of place. I settled for any kind of attention and as a result, I attended my senior prom with a guy who was beyond weird. He wore a pink-and-white tuxedo, and right in front of my parents, he tried to plant a big, wet kiss. Talk about brave or stupid.

The Beach Boys, Chicago, Jethro Tull, and Elton John concerts were at the top of the event list. Music had become my escape, and I owned every popular vinyl album and 45, with a terrific stereo system, head phones, and a yellow beanbag chair. I even had my own push-button phone, with a number I still remember. My bedroom was my haven of rest, and music was my safe place. At the time, I was also attending another denominational youth group that had teenage parties that were considered wild. But since I attended the LC on Sundays, I was more and more pressed inside that these parties were deeply wrong.

My identity of being gay started to move to the forefront in a subtle shift that had been secretly awakened by the girl in the neighborhood a few years earlier. But now it started to take shape in my fantasy life as I listened to music about love. I did not want the love of a man—I secretly desired the love of a woman. This scared me, as I had entirely too much biblical teaching to even remotely justify that it was an acceptable direction. I had not fully committed to the LC but was attending once a week. During the week, I participated in another church's youth-group sports and the wild weekend parties. The contrast between the wild youth group and the LC and the dilemma of sexual identity overwhelmed me. I relished the times where I could just hide in my bedroom, shut out the noise in my head, and let the music scream the words I could not say.

On my eighteenth birthday, my mom purchased a cake with a race car on the front. The driver was a girl with long black hair blowing in the wind, free as a bird. It was supposed to represent me. The LC young people had invited me to one of the communal houses to celebrate. After they sang "Happy Birthday," one of the young brothers in the group took a knife and scraped off the icing that was the head of the girl driving. He cut the head off and looked me straight in the eye. "You are here and won't need your mind anymore." I simply chuckled in my own survival way, unable to comprehend what had just occurred. The rest of the event was a blur, as I had shut down.

Shortly after, I was invited to a party with the youth group. That night I went into the backyard, sat on a hill, and consumed almost a fifth of vodka. I was only one hundred and ten pounds dripping wet. I went into the garage and told someone that I thought I was drunk. Approximately twenty hours later, I woke up on that garage floor, sick as a dog. Some of the other kids drove me home and had to stop about every two blocks while I vomited on the curb. I didn't know if I had a death wish, was just fed up, or was crying for help. My identity was gone, and I was completely lost, with no hope.

I arrived home, and there was no hiding this from my mother. I believed I was at death's door and completely poisoned with alcohol. I said to my mom, "I think I am just plain filled up and disgusted with everything."

She was actually pleased, as it had been an answer to prayer that I would consecrate myself to Christ. The next day was Saturday evening, and I attended a potluck at the LC. These folks met almost every day! During the meeting and the worship, I realized my life was a train wreck. I was staring in the face of a sexual identity that was off limits, I could not reconcile Christianity with wild parties, and the walls of protection had seemingly tumbled. The Lord gripped my heart to seek Him, and I called upon Him in a deep way. I was baptized in response to my rededication to God. It was a turning point. The cheers could have been heard throughout the city because I represented the prodigal daughter in their minds.

I perceived this LC to be the kind of encasement I required to protect me from myself. Instead I was on the verge of leaping into a vortex that would spin me for years to come.

Chapter 4

The Hammer of Compliance

S ubsequent to my baptism, the sisters sat me down and indicated that my clothing was becoming a distraction to the brothers in the church. I did not dress inappropriately, but I was not frumpy. Clearly, I stood out. This put me in a quandary, because now I had to fit in to ensure attention was replenished.

That night my mom said she would pay me one dollar for every article of clothing I threw in the trash. Back then one dollar per article, combined with a closetful of clothes, was a ton of money. *With such sacrifice, I would certainly get huge accolades from everyone,* I thought.

At the direction of the sisters, I also had to cut off all my "worldly" friends. At this crux, the bridge to the outside world was crumbling, and I had only one choice, other than drowning—make my home on the island of the LC and never look back. Once on that island, a journey back to my previous life would be nearly impossible, and all of reality would change instantaneously. After fifteen minutes of pondering, my decision was set: clear out the closet and retain only the clothes that had been shoved to the back for being out of style. I scored with lots of money that night, yet a large piece of me also went into the trash way ahead of God's timing and transforming work. Part of my identity was my apparel. My insides had been shattered, so all I had was the outward covering to look halfway decent to the rest of the world. That night I lay in bed feeling naked and uncovered, and I envisioned in horror wearing the frumpy clothes that had narrowly escaped the trash bin.

The summer after graduation, my participation in LC life accelerated, and I was fully dipped and soaked in the environment. My clothes had gradually altered, and I even had my own head covering and little towel to place over my legs during services. But I was still living at home with a level of safety.

College loomed on the horizon, and I had no clue what I wanted to study. I had received a scholarship from UCLA but turned it down for two reasons. First, the school scared me. It seemed so advanced, and I felt so young. Second, the LC did not look favorably on educational advancement toward a career. As a result, I was headed to Cal State Northridge with no direction. The common career aspirations of the LC included pool men or gardeners, and for many of the young sisters, housecleaning. Education was seen as a worldly endeavor, but my mother had instilled in me at a young age, and repeated it throughout the years, I was to get an education so I would not have to depend on anyone for my future or my existence. This was embedded in my core.

Just prior to my first semester in college, I was approached to move into a "sisters' house." The house had about ten other sisters, and the homeowners were the main elder of the church and his wife. I was thrilled at the prospect because it implied instant friends. Many of the occurrences in the church and the experiences of a young person were hidden from the parents. My mother's heart was protection for me, and this LC seemed to be the best option based on where I was headed as a teenager. My parents agreed to pay my living expenses while I attended college. The icing was that I was in the number one home that all the sisters vied for. I was chosen—wow!

A horizontal identity (based purely on human relationships and defined by their perceptions of me) was being molded and reinforced at a rapid pace. Gaining my identity from God, a vertical alignment, was a foreign concept and not an identification that I perceived yielded much benefit. People had become my litmus test, and therefore, people must be the ones to please.

I packed all my things, excited for this new freedom and adventure. The sisters' house was walking distance from the LC. I had my little white VW for transportation elsewhere. Since I was limited in the items I could bring to my new home, my tennis racket, Schwinn bike, bowling ball, records, and stereo equipment remained at my parents' house.

I moved in with the others and shared a Spartan room with two sisters. Closet space was at a premium, and the area could support only a little desk and dresser. No pictures or decorations graced the room, and the bedding was plain. Nothing reflected any personality, in contrast to the bedroom I had left.

Within a few short days, the LC rules became obvious. Though unspoken rather than in a policy document, they represented the culture and environmental norms that determined acceptance or rejection and praise or chastisement:

- No TV or radio of any kind
- No entertainment
- No dating or contact with the opposite sex
- No reading of any material other than life-study messages by Witness Lee or Watchman Nee or the Bible
- No sports or activities deemed worldly (This implied everything.)
- No photographs
- No friendships (They were from the soul and worldly. The church emphasized living in our spirit where the "Holy Spirit" resides, so mind, emotion, and will had no place. Since friendships encompassed an emotional and psychological component, they had to be abandoned to allow our spirit to thrive unencumbered.)
- Live in our spirits and forget our minds (this implied that school was unimportant and only led to worldly gain.)

No friendship. I had moved into a home perceiving I would gain friends and relationships. That could not have been further from the truth.

For a number of months, I refused to abide by the rules, and it became apparent I had dropped into a religious hell. All the bridges off this island had been burned. As I looked out over the dark sea of my life, the links to my past were fading into a deep fog. I could not ask my parents to rescue me, as they were in the church as well. Additionally, the LC had become a pseudo identity, and the mother of my new home, Vee, bewitched me.

Vee was extremely strict. Every morning at 5:30, we had to rise, smiling, for morning watch, in which we pray-read the Word. In this area I followed along perfectly, yet I was not experiencing any life in the Word. I became Vee's favorite, but I was also frightened because I witnessed her wrath toward young women who did not "keep in time" with the rules set forth. I never knew where I stood with Vee, as she was kind one minute and terrifying the next. Every time I stepped out of the house, I was sure a plan was being hatched to get rid of me. I lived in fear and insecurity and lay awake at night conjuring ways to stay in her good graces.

She claimed with her mouth she loved me, but everything else conveyed otherwise. That home was riddled with emotional dishonesty. Rejection by her, as a leader in the LC, had a more dramatic effect than the rejection and dismissal of a parent. Although I graduated with honors from high school, my first year of college was a miserable failure. Even the identity I had secured in grades was being annihilated.

Six months into my stay at the sisters' house, the big bomb dropped. LC leaders met with me and indicated I was not good enough, because I had failed to dispose of everything. Some clothes I owned were still unacceptable, and they challenged me to adopt new styles because the brothers were too distracted. Of course they were. I was one of the few who actually washed her hair on a regular basis and still wore a bit of makeup, but I didn't dress immodestly.

The sisters made it seem as if I had a choice, but in reality I had no choice. I was nineteen years old, and this had become my new world. Church was held almost every night of the week, and sometimes the services lasted for hours. I was already broken to a large degree and even stopped feeling the effects of diabolical hammering on my soul.

At San Pedro beach, people could build fires inside the mountain in creative fire pits. They were large, like tunnels. Every so often, the LC had "burnings." They planned them when the influx of new people had reached critical mass.

The timing of the conversation with the leading sisters about my failure to dispose of everything and the resulting distraction of the brothers was only three weeks before the next burning. I was a good soldier in God's army and God's recovery, on a mission to be the *best* soldier and a star young person.

I drove to my parent's home and gathered up everything I had left behind in the move to the sister's house: my stereo equipment, my records, clothing items I hadn't been able to part with previously, picture albums, high school albums and memorabilia, my bike, my tennis racket, my bowling ball, my jewelry from my mom and my grandma (valuable, I might add), portable radios, posters, makeup, and anything else not tied down. I was also supposed to write a note with my name on it and toss it into the flames as a representation that I was throwing *me, my sinful self,* into that fire as well.

The LC brothers secured a little truck to transport my belongings, while I drove behind in my VW bug. That day I wore the few items I had left: blue turtleneck, jean skirt, and sandals. My hair felt greasy, as we'd had to get up early. I felt constricted in my clothes because all we did was eat at the sisters' house. Just pray and eat—but not much love! (To this day, I cannot bear tight clothing, as it takes me back to this day on the beach.)

It was eighty degrees on that California coastline. I looked out at the sand and thought, *What has happened?* Just two years ago I'd been wearing a bikini and lying on a similar beach, enjoying the sun and my friends.

The ritual began. I was the only one who had mountains of items, so the cheers of praises to God rang out as I tossed things into this raging-hot fire. I was already too warm in my clothes, so the heat just about did me in. My emotions overwhelmed me. Time had stopped. Cari was gone. It was as if the noise around me was "blah, blah, blah." I could not believe my eyes as I witnessed my entire life from age zero to nineteen going up in flames. The worst tragedy of it all—I had no deep personal reality of Christ. This was not Christ's doing. If it had been, deep joy would have been the outcome of obedience to Him. (I can say this with confidence, as there have been things over the last few years that, in obedience to His speaking, I have purged. Those occasions have *never* been followed by regretful loss.)

Depression and sadness did not adequately describe what occurred that day. As I headed back to my VW, I thought, *Well, at least I have my car radio.* That same strange thought hit another brother, and next thing I knew they were removing my dashboard. They tossed it into the ocean with my bowling ball, which did not seem to burn fast enough.

I felt God had left and I had no one. I was not even able to cry, as that would be an expression of emotion and flesh. I could not share my pain with a friend, because that was considered "soulish." Even my happy place in my mind—the place of no noise, no rules, beautiful music, feeling the ocean breeze, running through tall grass barefoot, and freely crying—was clouded by the smoke of the fire that day.

After that I excelled in the LC and learned how to play guitar so I could qualify for the worship team. Targeted as a high-potential young person in the Lord's recovery, I was also asked to share the messages on Sunday mornings. Witness Lee wrote life-study booklets that were about thirteen pages long. Our job was to memorize those life-study pages before Sunday morning and spit it back with all the vigor and excitement we could muster. Fortunately, I had somewhat of a photographic memory, so my ability to assimilate and picture helped me greatly. I would stand in the middle of the circle, preaching with all the appropriate inflections and hand gestures to incite the masses toward praise. I excelled in this, so I was called upon frequently for this task. I had minimal personal reality of the Bible commentary I was conveying, yet it fed my pride massively and fed that horizontal identity. (In the context of God's sovereignty, I was receiving accelerated training for public speaking. Based on my heart for the Gospel, I know God has used, and will use, this for His purpose.)

About a year later, the LC experienced an influx of hippie-type people. I was thrilled, as they were intriguing and different and not afraid to be my friend. Unfortunately, the women I considered the coolest had sexual identity issues as well. We would gather together and have fantastic guitar jams, singing and praising Jesus. Love just filled the room. It felt so free, and many times I enjoyed the Lord. I was able to speak to these women in a real way, and freely given hugs were commonplace. I wanted it to last forever.

Then the gauntlet dropped. The so-called scandal was brought to the attention of the elders, and all hell broke loose—there were homosexuals in the midst. Vee, the queen mother, was tasked with dealing with these girls. In complete distress, I watched out my bedroom window as they stood on the curb graciously and humbly accepting the verbal beating from Vee. I cried as these humiliated girls drove away, never to return.

I'd figured out exactly what my struggle was and finally called myself gay, though not audibly, of course. I was safe, though, because no one would ever suspect. I did not look gay, per the world's impressions. When Vee subsequently stomped into the house and spit on the ground, horror seized me, and I hated her in my heart. Yet even with the hate, I needed her to love me, I needed her attention, and I needed her to approve of me, so my secret needed to be kept locked. This furthered the compelling requirement to keep in time with the rules.

Many of the young people went to Cal State Northridge, so I could not even escape at school. I was required to gather with them on breaks and lunch. We even had Gospel marches with drums and horns, where we all wore white robes and marched around campus, saying, "Christ and the church are taking the earth." We also strutted up and down neighborhoods like little soldiers.

After my first two years of college, I had no clue about a major and decided to take a trip with the church to Asia—Taiwan, Hong Kong, the Philippines, Korea, and Japan. It was good timing, as my grades were horrible. I had massive stress, and I functioned in continual survival mode. The places we would tour were key stakeholder territories for the LC, as Witness Lee had come from China.

It was my first time out of the country, and I was a young twenty-year-old psychologically. I traveled with another sister in the church, Lana, who had serious struggles. We were friends to a degree, but guarded. We loved each other, and given the right circumstances might have acted on it, but the boundaries of the church were so intense and scary that we would have never defied the rules. We were both little stars.

Upon arrival in Asia, we were escorted to a home where no one spoke English. While lying in the bed that night, I felt intense loneliness combined with a high fever. I cried out to God to heal my fever, similar to a young child pleading for help, not even knowing if anyone heard. But God heard, and little did I know that His healing of that fever would represent a picture of the healing of my being that would transpire years later. I woke up the next morning feeling perfect and knew Jesus had answered my simple prayer.

The eight weeks of subsequent travel were nothing short of taxing. Church meetings every night, food that was unidentifiable, and a constant discomfort in my clothes. Bathing was a challenge, as I had long hair and it sometimes fell into the tub drain, which was connected to the sewer system just inches below the surface.

Some of the meetings had ten thousand people in attendance, all yelling "O Lord Jesus" and "We are the Lord's recovery."

Joining the trip were some interesting folks from other parts of the United States. They had a rebellious streak, and their leader was not on board with Witness Lee being God's man on earth. It was as if a Judas had snuck into the camp, as this leader was one of Witness Lee's right-hand men. When on the bus, this contingency shared about freedom and how we were not under law but under grace, but they were not speaking of a grace constrained by love for God. This grace implied throwing caution to the wind. Someone on the team overheard this and reported it as a poison. (A few years later, this poison manifested itself in a huge way at a frenzy fest in Berkeley, followed by a harsh rebuke from Witness Lee, who phrased it as "a black spot on the Lord's recovery." I personally embraced the mini rebellion and stood front and center at the Berkeley free-for-all.)

I survived the Asia trip but returned home extremely sick. As a consequence of poor diet, I had dropped to ninety-five pounds dripping wet. The waistline of my skirt had to be cinched with a little rope for the plane ride home. I experienced no clothing constriction that day.

Although this was my first overseas trip, it was also God's preparation for the many trips to come down the road and numerous opportunities to preach the gospel message. It trained me to be brave and flexible in the harshest of circumstances.

My vacations in the LC encompassed ten-day trainings on a particular book of the Bible. These non-optional trainings occurred three times per year and were attended by LC people from all over the world. Three meetings were held each day, and churches were randomly called upon from the different cities to be tested on the prior meeting's content. It was draining, with no nap or sleep in between—just an intense study of notes to make sure every point was exact. A specific training on Hebrews left a scar. Our LC was called for testing, and for some reason I was selected to answer the question. I had studied but was incredibly nervous. I responded but did not get it exact, and Witness Lee pointed his finger at me and said, "Wrong. Go back. Someone else answer." The shame and embarrassment just made me want to throw the Bible on the floor. I felt as if I were being force fed, and given that I had head understanding and minimal internal reality of what I was reading, I crumbled under the pressure.

My mother, who saw this episode, attempted to provide comfort, but I was devastated and inconsolable. I did not reveal the level of pain outwardly, but I was surprised the bed sheets were not stained that night as my soul bled out from such deep rejection inflicted by the one who held the highest honor in the LC.

I dreaded these trainings. The seats were too close together, the room was hot, and I felt constricted. The walls were closing in, and I could barely breathe.

Lana and I lived in the same sisters' house. We played guitar in the service and had been earmarked as high-potential young people. Ironically, we never competed. We were always together and were nicknamed the dynamic duo. Even churches in other cities knew of us.

Sometimes we snuck out of the sisters' house at about 10:00 p.m. and walked for miles just to feel the air and taste a brief sense of freedom. We laughed like five-year-olds and skipped down the street, singing. A couple of times we were spotted by police cars going the other direction, and we ran like mad and leaped into the bushes. Fortunately, we were never picked up. Quite a thrill! We made sure we were back in time to throw on our pajamas and get downstairs for morning watch at 5:30 a.m.

Chapter 5

Road Trips and the LC Marriage

Shortly after I returned home from Asia, my mother had a serious car accident. As a result, it seemed best for me to move home, and Lana moved in with my parents too. Vee was not happy that the two stars were moving out, though I had been getting a bit gutsy and had said some hurtful things. However, God ordered the move. I had returned to college and decided on a major in business. The move alone was instrumental in my grades skyrocketing, as I was free from Vee.

Lana became neurotic and emotionally unpredictable. I realized that the LC was not helping the broken—rather, it was simply perpetuating the brokenness. Poor Lana was one of the broken too.

She and I took two road trips to see the LCs in different cities, as they had become prolific. We traveled up the West Coast and across the country to Oklahoma. We drove my little Dodge Colt and were like two lost children trying to find our way. We set up camp in the most unlikely places and were entirely too brave, or ignorant. On one occasion, we arrived in a pitch-black location. We set up our tent on this soft grassy field with wide-open spaces, and the stars were out en masse. The next morning the golfers arrived ahead of our wake-up time. We about went into shock as we scrambled to gather our things. (I golf now, and to this day when I see an area similar to the one where we stayed, I smile inside.)

We took our guitars on those trips and would sing the night away in freedom and joy. I believed God showed up in the midst of our worship. God also guarded us, as the homosexual struggle was massive.

Over time, Lana had opened up to me about being adopted and the horrible abuse she had experienced. I tried desperately to fix her, not realizing I was also the perfect train wreck. So there we were, two kids at twenty trying to swim through a mess as the mud stuck to our hands like putty and refused to let go. I never acted on my struggle with her, or even broached the subject verbally, as the fear of the LC far outweighed any propensity to satisfy physical needs or reveal psychological secrets.

We lived with my parents for a year and moved back to a sisters' house. Lana and I were separated, which at this point was a positive thing. I was blessed and fortunate to land in the home of Buck and Verba, a couple who knew the Lord intimately and believed fully in the freedom and liberty in Christ. They were like grandparents to me. When I would launch into well-rehearsed religious rhetoric, Verba would simultaneously pick up her wooden spoon, shake it, and say, "No, no, no." In that home I experienced Christ in some honest settings. The couple provided an example of Christ's love in the midst of the prison that had entrapped me and stolen my youth.

I had some fun roommates, and it was the setting God ordered for me to finish college. Thankfully, I pulled up all my grades and completed college with high honors. Based on my grades of the first two years, this was a true miracle.

The courtship and marriage framework was rather peculiar in the LC. No one dated, and there were no long conversations with the opposite sex—actually, no conversation. A brother simply expressed interest in a sister to the elders. The term was coined "a burden," but in reality might have been more like "lust." The elders would agree to pray. Once they validated the burden in their own minds, they approached the sister. If she acknowledged interest, away the new couple went. No, not dating, but meeting together under supervision. The announcement of an engagement to the rest of congregation was simply the pair's planned first-time walk into the church together. But they did not sit together. The engagements were not long, about two months maximum. A wedding feast was held, with testimonies and loads of "praise the Lord" from the bride and groom. (Unfortunately, many of those marriages have ended in divorce.) A considerable number of young people also struggled with their sexuality. Additionally, marriage was the only way of an authorized encounter with the opposite sex. Such were the ingredients for ultimate disaster.

In the summer between age twenty-one and twenty-two, the burdens for me were being requested steadily. Not that I was such a prize, but I was still a little star. I washed my hair on a regular basis and kept my weight in check despite all the eating and praying. I did not hear about the dialogues, as the elders never approached me to solicit my "yes" or "decline." They wanted to preserve me.

My mother revealed this some years later. This was also God's hand, as any one of those brothers would have been awful. Many had gone to college just to share the Gospel. They took random classes with no direction, which I found rather ridiculous. (Almost all of them are long gone from the LC, and worse, gone from God.)

One thing I refused to do was let these elders pick for me. When I was twenty-two, a young man walked into the LC. He was absolutely adorable with his long, wavy hair, French-cut T-shirt, and a smile like there was no tomorrow. He was a safe choice because I sensed he struggled with my same homosexual issue. The next time I saw him, his hair was cut and he had on the infamous costume of the brothers, collared shirt and khaki pants. *That certainly did not take long*, I thought. He was going to be a teacher and also attended Cal State Northridge. At age twenty-three, I decided I wanted to get married. Clearly, graduating from college and getting married were the natural courses of life.

I was still living with Buck and Verba and indicated to them my interest in the new young man, Peter. The information was transmitted to the elders, and shortly thereafter Peter called me, reciprocating interest. He would come over to the sisters' house for dinner, and we had a great time visiting. He was kind, loving, and studying for a bachelor's degree. Although he wore the costume of the brothers, his shirts were always pressed and his pants were the proper length. Verba even did some of his alterations. We did go out and spend time together on our own, much to the chagrin of some. One time he dropped me off at my home, and I wondered if he even knew how to kiss. I was pleasantly surprised.

He spent all his money to buy me a ring and shared about his prior experiences in the gay life and his engagement to a woman, which had fallen apart when she was diagnosed with cancer. I was comfortable with all of it yet never shared that I struggled too. Marriage would fix everything. I did not carry some weird concept that I would be the perfect wife to fix him. I was more concerned about fixing me.

We graduated together at the end of May 1981 and were married on June 6 that year. Our marriage was the beginning of our journey, as we would both make the great escape from the sister and brother homes, live on our own, and start work in the real world. I did not know what "in love" was, so I made tremendous mistakes along the way. Two broken people coming together in a marriage with little resolved at the core, each with a sexual identity struggle, led to a myriad of complications in the midst of some wonderful times.

Chapter 6

The Great Escape

Peter and I lived in a cute apartment filled with refinished garage sale furniture. With my bachelor's degree in business, I landed a terrific job as a management trainee at a large computer printer company. Although Peter had secured a degree in liberal studies with a goal to be a teacher, he decided early on that teaching was not going to cut it economically. Instead he secured a banking position that paid for his master's degree.

Both of us were burned out on the LC, though we never spoke about it bluntly. The work environment offered the first bridge of hope off the little island. We interfaced with people who were not part of the LC. I started dressing professionally, and at a gradual pace, my closet altered in style. It was not a dramatic overnight change—more like systematic, deliberate, and with extreme caution. I kept the frumpy clothes so I could look the part when we went to the meetings.

A fear element was associated with leaving the LC. One was considered poisonous if he or she spoke anything in disagreement to the LC life. In an attempt at mind control, many stories were told about people dying of lawn mower cord electrocution or random bizarre accidents because they had left the Lord's recovery.

Noise traveled through the LC that Peter and I were on the verge of defecting. That created another frightening strain. Although those in the LC were not friends per se, they were still the go-to people, as I had not found solid "transport" off the island yet. I didn't know if I was more afraid of them or of God.

Peter and I had acquired cars that had radios. I tested God many times by turning it on for five minutes. If I did not have a car accident, I left it on for another five minutes. Soon I grew comfortable and let it blast and felt free to fly.

People at work talked about TV shows. We did not have a TV, but that soon changed, and I was glad we did not die after the purchase. One night though, I tried my hand at cooking fried eggplant. Not the most skilled cook, I was not adept on how to combat a grease fire. I had long black hair and was wearing a robe. All of a sudden, the frying pan caught on fire. I picked it up and put it under water. I didn't know how that fire went out and the place didn't burn down with me inside. I believed Jesus had stepped in and protected me. The fire alarms shrieked in the building, and fear overwhelmed me, as I thought this was punishment. Since we had little money, I asked the landlord if I could refinish the cabinets, and ironically, they came out better than when we'd moved in. God's grace for certain, as we were poor but happy. The event, though, gave me pause. I did not turn on the radio or TV for a while.

Peter and I excelled in our positions and started making decent money. He was gone many evenings, and I worked for an older woman named Sally. She was the epitome of the businesswoman who had gone through the hard knocks of women's liberation. Even though the war had been won, she still had the battle weapons ready to fire. She took me under her wing and gave me my first management position at the ripe age of twenty-seven, reporting directly to her. Sally dressed like a million dollars, wore makeup perfectly, and walked like she owned the place. She was feared by many, but I liked her. She was Russian and had class (at least, the way I defined class).

Up to this point, our pace of exit from the LC was subtle yet steady. We had great excuses—working, studying, and newly married. But when Sally entered the scene, my "transportation" arrived! I jumped into my speedboat with the accelerator pressed to the floor and waved goodbye to that little LC island. I set my sights on the prospect of freedom, and I was mesmerized by my new object of affection: Sally. Unfortunately, in my hearty wave goodbye, I also waved goodbye to God. He had become disguised by all the legalism and treachery. As far as I was concerned, He was cruel, unloving, undesirable, and a thief of my youth. Peter's sentiments were not as dramatic. His experience in the LC was considerably less in years as well as impact. Still, we shut the door on the LC as a unified force, and we shut it hard.

Peter made new friends, and some were entrenched in astrology, crystals, chart readings, and other New Age elements that posed as many roads leading to God. In contrast to the LC, the concept of *friendship* was embraced. They were nonjudgmental and the opposite of harsh and legalistic. Our circle expanded as we attended corporate events and engaged with normal people. I felt like I had been in a coma, losing years in the LC, and when I woke up out of the fog, the world had moved on. Daunted by all I had missed— movies, shows, songs, artists, the college experience—deep resentment settled in my heart, as those years were unrecoverable. Therefore, I jumped in to embrace the world and all it had, on a mission to recapture lost time.

Sally and I often went out after work for drinks, sometimes three times a week. She taught me drinking and driving skills that were dangerous and plain stupid. By the grace of God, I always made it home and never hurt anyone or got arrested. We shared deep vulnerabilities, yet many times she would forget them the next day. This frustrated me, as I recollected everything. Sometimes I would not get to bed until 2:00 a.m. and then would rise again at 8:00 a.m. the next day, excited to go into the office and see her.

Sally taught me style and guided me on how to select my first grown-up bra at a classy boutique. She taught me the art of makeup, and when I waltzed into the office with my new look, coworkers were astounded. I walked on air. I looked fine with jewelry, new clothes, and a pep in my step. God, however, was far from view.

My boss became a big part of my world, and Peter knew it. Yet he was also living in his compartmentalized world of survival and was gone most nights for schooling, so we made few demands on each other, especially in the arena of physical intimacy. We had lots of wonderful times though. He is Italian, so I was instantly transported into this big infrastructure. My immediate family was small in comparison, so the inheritance of new brothers, sisters, and in-laws was spectacular, family dynamics and all.

Peter and I purchased a home across the street from his brother. The home was a catastrophe when we bought it, but Peter had a vision, and that little home became our first palace. A few years later we moved to our dream home in Simi Valley. Although Peter had abandoned his love of the cello, it did not alter the fact that he was a gifted musician. We attended ballets, opera, live theater, and concerts on a regular basis, with a potpourri of friends. We loved to shop, and as a double-income, no-kids couple, clothes shopping sprees were commonplace. We enjoyed the malls and knew how to spend money.

Eventually, Sally was integral to both our lives. Peter had met her husband at one of the corporate events, and the four of us hit it off. They introduced us to their favorite Russian supper club, which we frequented on a regular basis. Eleven courses of delectable foods and dancing the night away to live music fed the passion and energy I had bottled up for years. We participated in weekend poker games while drinking shots of all the flavors of Stolichnaya vodka. It was a time of decadence, and I was free. No boundaries, no hindrances, and no relationship with God seemed the ideal ingredients of the happiness meal for the starving soul.

One of the people Peter embraced was a man named Rick, a client of Peter's at the bank, and Peter invited him to our home for dinners and other get-togethers with friends. I later determined that Rick prayed to the god of this world, Satan. We were invited to his home for a dinner engagement. A few days earlier, I had been in bed sick and happened upon a Geraldo show about Satan worship in the United States. The program displayed many of the symbols and even the construct of occultist altars. The visions stuck in my mind. God ordained for me to see this. We arrived at Rick's home, and the minute I walked in the door, I saw the same things. I shook inside and knew he was not a safe man. I also took a pause, although brief at that time, on where I was headed. I had abandoned God, and I questioned my faith. Was I really that much different from Rick? Whom was I serving?

Before I left on a business trip to Ireland, Rick asked me to bring back a leprechaun figurine. I complied even though I thought he was off his rocker. When I gave it to him, I thought that was the end, but apparently he took it home, blessed it, and then returned it to me. I did not think much about it, as I was fond of the little statue. I placed it on the bar in our home and forgot about it until one night I woke up startled and thought I was seeing ghosts in my bedroom. I knew what I saw, and it was evil. Even though my walk was far from God, I was seized by the Lord to shatter that little "innocent" leprechaun with no delay. I went downstairs and smashed it to pieces. At that juncture, the Lord stirred in me that we had gone too far and had opened doors that were leading to dark places. I wondered if in leaving the LC, we had thrown out the baby with the bathwater.

In the meantime, I discovered Sally was a full-blown alcoholic. The relationship confused and tormented me, as I was so utterly attached. When her husband died suddenly, our relationship escalated, not in a physical way, but psychologically as I gradually discovered her own torment and hell in the marriage and tried to be there for her. While helping her clean house, the amount of weird and dark paraphernalia uncovered from secret hidden cubbies would make the average person run for their life. My conscience knew this was bad stuff, but I was too attached to exit the relationship.

After a few years, the work setting combined with the friendship became a hard task to balance. This was further complicated when another manager entered the scene, clearly broken in a similar manner to me, yet older and married as well. She created a triangular mess and a complete psychological drain on my system. The relationship with Sally diminished. But by the grace of God, a gal I worked with had watched the dynamics from afar and had been in Al-Anon.

Chapter 7

"Twelve Steps" Closer and True Friendship

The complex relationship with Sally only furthered my plight with sexual identity. Combined with her alcoholism, the experience swirled into a confusing and psychological mess. She eventually remarried, and I moved on to another role in the company. Although I tried to keep the relationship alive, God had something much different in mind.

Al-Anon is where friends and families of alcoholics learn to deal with their own codependent behaviors, taking the focus off the alcoholic and working on their own personal issues. It's a powerful twelve-step program designed to bring wholeness and health to those who have suffered and endured in relationships with alcoholics. Initially, I wasn't sure why I was there. I just knew my friend had watched the dynamics between Sally and me, and I decided it would be good for me.

Al-Anon welcomed newcomers, and I had never heard the twelve steps. The concept intrigued me, so I attended a few times. I met a dear woman named Maria, who displayed the light of the Lord in a way I had never seen. I was so drawn to her freedom and her smile that I asked her to be my sponsor. I was her first "baby," a term used to describe the sponsor-sponsee relationship.

The people in the group had a variety of higher powers, and that subject was not probed much. Maria and I became close, so I directly asked her to define her higher power. She said the Gospel was front and center in her life and she fully embraced the cross of Christ and redemption. I was so excited I could barely contain it, and the sharing continued into the wee hours of the night. The seed of Christ was in my life, but I'd tried to pour concrete over it when I left the LC. The Lord's seed in me leaped in connection with the Lord in her, in spite of my hearty fights against Him. Thankfully, that seed had an unseen, underground, live-root structure that no human antics could destroy. Unfortunately, there were still many years left before greenery would appear.

I attended the Al-Anon meetings as often as possible. The group was such a contrast to the LC. These people revealed their hearts. Friendship and love flowed. One could be safely vulnerable, and I did not hesitate to share my life and struggles.

In the course of all of this, Peter did his thing. Our double income increased at a rapid pace, and we traveled on many vacations. All seemed well. However, his sexual identity struggle had heightened. I felt rejected—not sexual rejection, as I did not have that kind of drive, but more the emotional rejection of hugs, friendship, and attention. I was anything but the perfect wife. We both were tangled up, and neither of us had the necessary tools to weave our way through the mess. No one would have ever guessed. But my sponsor, Maria, knew, although nothing specific was ever discussed.

I grew spiritually to some degree in Al-Anon, but my sexual identity struggle loomed in the shadows. Sometimes Peter or I would comment, in a joking manner, when we spotted an attractive man or woman. Although never talked about, we intuitively knew the same-sex attraction existed in each of us. Therefore, our marriage relationship had an element of safety.

After one of my last meetings in Al-Anon, I arrived at home late at night. Peter had been gone on a fishing trip, but he had returned home earlier that same day. The front of the house was dark. I walked through the front entryway into the living room and closed the door behind me. Immediately, I heard a little knock. Without thinking, I opened the door, and the next thing I knew I had a knife at my neck. Paralyzed, I could not speak or scream. Peter had just given me the most beautiful emerald ring, and all I could do was clench my fists.

Peter wandered to the front room, intending to greet me. Stunned to discover I was not alone, he belted out a scream, "What the $$@# are you doing with my wife?"

Startled, the man ran out the door to the golf course.

Peter looked at me and said, "Call 911." He raced out in his underwear to chase this perpetrator.

I stayed calm as I dialed the phone and relayed the story. But when the police showed up, so did an adrenaline rush, and the pain coursing through my entire body was almost unbearable.

As the events were conveyed, the police indicated that the house had probably been watched for a few days. Had Peter not been home, this story might have had a much different end and my life might have been cut short. I will never know. One thing is certain—the living God protected me. What frightened me most was that I'd had no voice and could not even scream. I'd gone limp like a little rag doll.

Peter and I loved and cared for each other, and it would have devastated him if that attack had resulted in a more tragic end.

As for me, it took about twenty years before the infrequent panic attacks stopped.

Chapter 8

A Beautiful Baby and a Liberal Family Structure

We'd been married eight years when Peter insisted it was time for a child. Peter had wanted a child from the beginning, but the drive heightened when he knew our marriage was on a thin thread because of his identity struggle. He had started therapy under the premise that he needed to work on himself. I did not challenge it, because I knew his upbringing had many complexities. On one level, he wanted to keep the family intact. I trusted him implicitly. On the flip side, I struggled with the proposition of a child, because so much of my youth had been taken, and at thirty years old, freedom was big in my mind. I was entrenched in my own selfish world and still a prisoner of my own loss of freedom as a result of the LC.

We had planned a five-week backpacking vacation to Europe, and Peter wanted us to toss precaution aside. Afraid, I struggled with the idea. But ... God!

It was March 1990 during Passover season. We'd been invited to a Jewish Seder. I was running late, so I stopped at a phone booth to call Peter. I stepped inside that little booth, made the call, hung up, and suddenly had a deep encounter with the Lord. Initially, it was more like a fight. I sat in the booth and cried in utter fear of having a child. I disagreed with His plan, and I fought hard to change His mind (which, by the way, *never* works). Ultimately, I surrendered and was sure I would get pregnant on the trip. I shared the story with Maria, my Al-Anon sponsor, and in her gracious words she said, "Cari, God obviously has a plan."

As we backpacked from country to country through Europe, Peter and I connected like never before. We were out of our normal Los Angeles environment and separated from the hidden parts of our dark lives, a true blessing. Sure enough, I came home and took the test. That big plus sign appeared, and reality hit. I was going to be a mom.

The first couple of months were uneventful, and then one day at the beach, while lying on my tummy, I felt this featherlike flutter and realized I had a life inside me. A flood of tears streamed down my cheeks. I knew intellectually the miracle of life, but now that miracle was a "felt" experience. I imagined what this baby would look and be like. I embraced the responsibility of taking excellent care of myself for the next remaining months to ensure this baby would be healthy and strong. Step aerobics, a healthy diet, and classical music were habits for the next several months. Peter and I talked to my tummy and stared in awe each time we viewed the ultrasounds and witnessed the miraculous progress of life.

On January 27, 1991, she popped out after three hours of labor. I guessed God remembered our battle in the phone booth, so He gave me an easy labor.

When Peter and I held this treasure who had been given to us, we decided that the next good thing for us all would be church. Given our history, we wanted our daughter, Elizabeth, to find Christ as well. Our lives had simmered down. We were in our early thirties and appeared stable as a couple. Peter still went to therapy, and I thought nothing of it and never questioned the subject matter, his progress, or why.

We tried out a large nondenominational church near our home and opted to attend on a regular basis. Elizabeth was just shy of her first birthday when we dedicated her to Christ on the platform of the church. We prayed, and the congregation prayed.

For the next two years, we raised our beautiful girl and went to church every Sunday. She was a huge blessing in our lives.

But our family structure teetered on the brink of destruction. One night, the reason for Peter's therapy burst forth in one fell swoop. He felt he needed to be true to himself and embrace his identity as a gay man. (By the grace of God, we were, and still are, both healthy and well, as our marriage years were during the height of tremendous tragedy among the gay community.) Peter had met a man and indicated he could no longer live a lie with me.

The news hit me like running into a brick wall or a sudden gunshot to the heart. Every emotion coursed through my body, including a sense of deep betrayal by Peter and by God. I had surrendered my life to have a child, and now I would be left alone as a single parent. I was still trying to figure out mommyhood, and I loved Elizabeth to pieces, yet fear pummeled me like an avalanche. I screamed, yelled, wept, and threw things in the privacy of my bedroom the night Peter left our home forever. Unlike the battle in the phone booth, this was all-out war with the Lord. Four hours of gut-wrenching tears and tremendous loss. When I finally ran out of steam and lay exhausted, something powerful occurred. I felt wrapped in the arms of Jesus, like I was in a cocoon of love. I knew He was there. In one astounding moment, I was calm, I could breathe, and my tears of anger turned to tears of surrender.

My request of the Lord over the next six months was to receive the gift of forgiveness. A key principle my mother had instilled in me regarding forgiveness as an imperative was about to be tested. I had watched people grow bitter and sick because they could not release and forgive, especially in Al-Anon. I knew I would be eaten alive if I clung to pain, and unforgiveness would be a poison in my soul.

Peter now lived at the beach and invited me to come and meet his new love, Jim. I wanted to find out about Jim since he would be part of Elizabeth's life. While driving on the 405 freeway, God granted my request. I was released from anger, and love filled my heart. Before I knocked on the door, I asked the Lord to go in before me and let me show grace. Although Elizabeth was only two, I knew my reaction would impact her as well.

The four of us had a delightful breakfast, and that would be the start of our three-person co-parenting experience.

Peter took me to a beautiful restaurant a few days later, and from the depth of his heart, he read me a touching letter of apology. We both sobbed. We not only loved each other, we also liked each other as dear friends.

We decided that throwing all the money into the air for attorneys to seize was foolish. Instead, we chose a mediator, who took us to lunch, and the entire divorce cost $700. We had assets, and we knew if we could not amicably divorce, we would never be capable of raising a child together. Although I had stopped going to Al-Anon, dear Maria was there by my side to walk me through this difficult time. I loved her heart and adored her walk with the Lord. She pointed me to Christ always!

I made a promise to my little girl that mommy would be by her side and it would be me and her against the world.

I hadn't anticipated that the divorce would trigger a tailspin. My own sexual identity struggle surged to the forefront like an uncontrollable beast.

Chapter 9

The Struggle Intensifies

To tame the beast, I dated men. My choices were deplorable. Even a dear friend said, "Cari, I think you are picking people who are completely out of the question." Even worse, I dated men while plagued with the fear of my same-sex attraction, which had not been addressed or healed, creating a toxic cocktail that ultimately put me in a deep depression.

I still had maintained my attendance at the church Peter and I had been attending and joined a singles group. I developed some wonderful friends, including a best friend. The singles group was terrific, with houseboat trips, country-western dances, cycling, swimming, and barbecues. A couple of gentlemen in the class wanted to date me, but I was not interested. They were good catches and even fairly well off, but I could not venture down that road. I did not feel safe, and I spent lots of energy to keep my own sexual struggle at bay.

A woman in the group, Pauline, was working toward her license to be a clinical therapist, and we became dear friends. Pauline, though, had some unhealthy practices. I had shared with her my sexual identity struggle, and she offered the crazy idea that she could provide counseling and remain a close friend. I was too ignorant to know the difference and was happy at the prospect of help.

We partied at dance clubs every week, and I became attracted to her. Then her new boyfriend started abusing her, and my therapy sessions shifted away from her helping me to me listening to and helping Pauline. So I gave her money and then counseled her.

Her boyfriend proposed marriage and threatened to expose her counseling practice if she did not cut things off with me. He knew the law, and she was clearly in violation by counseling someone and then engaging them as a friend the rest of the week. He also did not like the fact that I had his number. Pauline and I did not have an intimate lesbian relationship, although emotionally I wanted to be the replacement for her horrific boyfriend. He treated her like garbage, and I used to fantasize that if she were my partner, I would treat her like a queen. I hated seeing her tears from the abuse, and his push/pull games and manipulation disgusted me. During breaks in their relationship, I encouraged Pauline. She would be temporarily strong and cut things off.

Her boyfriend knew that I fed her the truth, and it maddened him. One day while witnessing him degrade Pauline, I told him exactly what I thought, an unwise decision given how emotionally locked in Pauline was to this man. This encounter, combined with his threats to expose her, resulted in a day where I lost a close friend and my therapist. She did not want to risk her license, and she did not want her coworkers to see me at the wedding. (Yes, she married the crazy man!) She had violated ethical and legal boundaries, and she worried that I might squeal. She stopped engaging with me on any level, as if I were the one who had committed the crime.

That dark time propelled me into a deeper state of despair. Many people advised me to press legal charges for her extreme ethical breach so that she would lose her license and never be able to act that way again. I could not do it, as I could have never lived with myself knowing I had destroyed another human being and her livelihood, even if I was well within my rights to do so. I am grateful for that decision. A number of months later, Pauline wrote me a heartfelt letter requesting forgiveness. I did forgive but never went back to the friendship, as the violation and hurt were too extreme.

Her marriage did not survive, and she finally escaped. *Therapy* became a dirty word in my vocabulary and was omitted from the list of helpful alternatives.

The one positive thing that came out of that trial, though, was the introduction to the Living Waters Program, which offered a place for people struggling with sexual identity who wanted to live God's way. I truly wanted to be healed, so I went for twenty weeks, four hours per week. For the first time I met people just like me, trying to navigate their way through Christianity in the midst of a dark secret. We sang worship songs each week for two solid hours, and joy filled my heart. Yet I found myself eyeing the females in the group and knew that this was a hopeless endeavor. My options for getting help were rapidly shrinking. Although I commended the program and had read of tremendous miracles, that was not my experience. But it did nourish the root structure of the seed of God inside me.

Some nights, I lay in my bed and cried. The pain inside and my desire for female love overwhelmed every part of my being like an all-consuming fire of passion that burned from the inside out. I sometimes thought I would die without it. Would the hole I had inside ever be filled? I would curl up in a fetal position and shake uncontrollably from the extreme pain.

Although attending a church and hearing great words of wisdom and going to wonderful conferences on prayer and wholeness, my personal walk with the Lord remained nonexistent. I spent no time with Him. The Bible was boring and lifeless. I knew God loved me, but the death of Jesus seemed ineffective. I felt that my deep struggle with homosexuality was left hanging on the cross, undefeated, while the rest of the plights of mankind were conquered mightily in the resurrection. I decided that the Lord had suffered a temporary blip when He formed me. It was as if all the other puzzle pieces were perfectly placed, but the ones in the center had gone missing somewhere in eternity past. I had lost all capacity to look back and see God's grace. The fear of the Lord and His Word was swallowed up by this untamable monster demanding to be fed. This wall encasing my heart blocked the Son, and the days became shorter and shorter until there was no day, just night.

Chapter 10

Jericho, My New Home

Now Jericho was tightly shut because of the
sons of Israel. No one went out and no one
came in.
*   —Joshua 6:1*

In the Bible, Jericho was a walled-in city. After God delivered the children of Israel from Egypt, certain cities had to be conquered in order for them to reach the land of promise that God had provided—the good land. Jericho was the strongest fortress, with a large wall surrounding it that stood between the Israelites and the good land. It was a self-contained bustling city. The Arabic meaning of Jericho is "city of the moon." The moon only derives its light from the sun. Given the height of the wall, many areas inside the city were likely shaded or dark most of the day.

A prostitute named Rahab had a home along the wall. She was trapped in her condition, yet she had heard the stories and knew about the God who had redeemed Israel and utterly destroyed Israel's enemies, which may have heightened her own fears. Joshua 2:11 says, "Our hearts melted and no courage remained." Freedom seemed impossible, and her destiny *appeared* set.

The next chapter in my own life would result in an entrapment like none other. The wall that had been built strengthened over time. This next phase would represent the ultimate shoring up. Inside my Jericho walls, I would be haunted by the knowledge of God's Word (which never returns void), by the realization of His past provision in my life, and by the intense fear that true freedom was never in the divine equation.

A Tragic Choice

I made a choice.

The devil did not make me do it. I made a conscious and deliberate decision that sent me spiraling into the pit of hell. I bought the lie that God had no power. I had experienced His deep love but not His resurrection power. I wrote a poem prior to entering my first gay bar. It's called "Unity of One," but in reality, it was the unity of me, myself, and I.

UNITY OF ONE

Slam the cell shut, close all the doors
Initiate the music from another score.
The voices scream, the voices shout
It's your demise if you let her out.
The dreams and hopes all fade away
My soul, the price required to pay.
Vulnerable eyes and a restless heart
Caressed each night as we live apart.
I fight with gusto and all of you cheer
Never recognizing the deep imbedded fear.
Only in my mind do we laugh and talk
Yet in such loneliness I am forced to walk.
Not the books nor the words teach me to love
The hole deep inside unknown to those above.
Busied and hurried I blast through this life
Yet you're in the shadows always there in my sight.
I reach out to hold you with all of my might
Yet visiting hours are only at night.
You are behind those detestable bars
So I race out of time where you're not so far.

Jericho, My New Home

Daylight has broken and I'm forced to hide
Wondering who will be at my side.
You are asleep and I feel you at peace
But why are you still so out of my reach?
I burn all I have and I rip you to shreds
Breaking the links from my heart to my head.
You never existed—"Oh you must not be"
Frenzied and guilty in my final plea.
I rage and I beat that huge part inside
Such tragedy in which you've been forced to abide.
I cry out in silence only to hear
A beckon and call saying, "Why do you fear?"
As I run to the place I left long ago
There you are waiting, the one that I know.
The path was not easy, storms in the way
But I understand the price I had paid.
Living a life behind walls of lies
No inner solace since breaking those ties.
The bars seem so strong, yet they melt right before me
I cry and I weep, as it's me that I see.
The collision is great in the quiet of my heart
Paint blends with canvas to create a new start.
We touch and we love finally walking as one
No need to hurry and no need to run.
The crowds and the voices dim with each breath
As my head, heart, and soul are joined at the depth.

This poem was birthed out of futility and despair. My insides were shattered, and I was on a mission to put them back together *my way*. I was determined to find, through another female, those puzzle pieces that God had omitted. Thus, the horizontal worship of the creature rather than the vertical worship of the Creator. The horizontal quest to find peace, love, joy, and completeness in a creature grew legs in the framework of a whole new race.

Family Reaction

My dear mom loved the Lord and loved me deeply. From the day I was born, she knew I belonged to the Lord and was simply a gift to her. Shortly after I met my first partner, I composed a letter to my mom and read it to her face to face. There was no shock, just love, and she wasn't surprised. My mom is wise, and she'd seen indicators. She had observed the relationship with Sally, and through Christ, Mom had a strong level of discernment that a struggle had been brewing. Yet she also had believed marriage had been a covering and protection.

My mother knew that only prayer and a deep encounter with the Lord would cause a course correction. She said few words. Homosexuality never became the central focus of our home or family events. She was not afraid of the subject and not embarrassed by it. Her close friends joined her in prayer. I did not upset the vision of the perfect family. My mother, from that time of my salvation at five and a half years old, had reminded me constantly that apart from Christ we humans were capable of anything under the sun, given the right circumstances. (I sometimes wonder if Christians truly acknowledge our fallenness and capacity for sin apart from God. How many believers would actually admit that "Yes, I am capable of homosexuality apart from Christ, given the right circumstances"?)

Her deep love also embraced whomever I loved. There were times when Mom would kindly question things, though she never told me what to do. I honored her home and would never ask to stay the night with a partner. My mother kept holiday meals and visits an open invitation. She never compromised her faith or her stance with the Word. She knew her commission was the prayer closet, and that she did on a daily basis.

When people asked my mother about me, she never said I was gay. She said I was struggling and needed desperate prayer. For my mom to say that "Cari is gay" would be to subvert and deny the *positional identity* that I had in Christ from the day I had received Him. (A citizen who takes the oath of enlistment becomes a member of the army, a soldier. When I received Christ, I instantly became a positional member of the body of Christ and belonged to Him. The positional identity was immediate and once and for all. A soldier's simple enlistment, however, does not translate into living, acting, and thinking like a soldier without practice and training in daily life. In the same manner, the end game of the Christian life is not simply positional. Although secure, it is just the beginning. Therefore, in this context, my mom knew that the proper noun to assign to me was *Christian* and the proper verb was *struggling*.)

My mom also passed the extreme test of forgiveness with Peter. She told him firsthand that she never had thought she had the capacity to kill anyone until he left our marriage. My mom was honest, but she put that honesty at the foot of the cross. As a result, she maintained a positive relationship with Peter that also included Peter's partner, Jim. Peter and Jim have never been outsiders.

My dear daughter, Elizabeth, was caught in the crossfire though. She was six when I met my first partner, and the mommy who had been attentive and promised her that it would be me and her changing the world started a redirection of focus that had a serious impact.

Chapter 11

Partner 1—Bea

On the night I drove to my first gay bar in North Hollywood, my whole being shook. Frightened yet exhilarated in anticipation of a relationship that would save my life forever, I walked in and sat at the bar like a kid in a candy store.

Bea was a lean and mean Puerto Rican with a pretty face and nice smile. She had just trekked across the country on her own to flee her past. We sat and talked for a long time, and I asked her out on a date. I counted down the days before I'd see her again. I was unable to concentrate at work, as thoughts of her consumed me. We were madly in love within two weeks, not an uncommon scenario among lesbians—the second date was usually a U-Haul truck. She quickly became my whole world and the object of my attention. Within six weeks, she had moved into my home.

Peter and I had shared custody of Elizabeth, so she was with Bea and me one full week and then transitioned to his house.

Bea had suffered under some harsh abuse as a child. The abandonment, rejection, and beatings inflicted from age three onward far outweighed any hardship I could claim. As a result, alcohol was her drug of choice. The many scars on her arms were the result of self-mutilation. She, too, had been dating men to no avail and one day decided to exit the scene and drive across country for a new life.

We locked in on the implied promise between two women: "You are promising me that you will fill in all the gaps of my lack. I am choosing *sameness* because my femaleness has a hole inside that can only fit another female. As a unit we will be a complete whole."

This implied promise was foundational to the survival of our relationship, as well as my future relationships. We were each other's first lesbian lover, and that had a passion and fire all its own. The first six months were like chocolate to my brain. I loved being in love, the greatest sensation of all. The Pepsi bottle had been sealed yet shaken violently over the years, and now the top popped off and I exploded with glee. My mom and Peter threw me a fortieth birthday party, and in many respects, it was also my coming-out party. Some attending grieved deeply, while others rejoiced over my newfound freedom.

Bea's insecurities unfolded in a dramatic way. They weren't as noticeable the first few weeks, but after she moved in, I was under the microscope. She started clocking the miles on my car, and she refused to allow me to carry any cash. She called me at work at least once per hour to see if I was there. I often went to the gym at lunch, and while I worked out, she would page me to make sure I was not at some hotel cheating on her. On any level, this was nothing like my marriage. I even lost control of the checkbook. We combined our finances, and she questioned every ATM transaction that was not her doing. I accommodated her and tried to make her secure. I was so addicted to her that I would do anything to prevent trouble or departure, yet it was to no avail, and things worsened. The glorious six months were up, and that implied promise vanished like the wind.

Her prized possession, her waterbed frame, sat in the garage because it would not fit inside my house. I arrived home one day, and she was destroying the waterbed with a chainsaw. My eyes were as big as saucers and nothing short of terrified as she screamed, "This is how much I love you." I guessed I should have been honored, but I just wanted to grab the chainsaw out of her hands. I had mastered the art of getting her off the wall. (A skill I use today in business on a much smaller scale, as, unfortunately, she afforded some of the greatest training.) Desperate, I thought it would be a great idea to bring God into the mix. I researched online and found a gay Christian church.

Since Los Angeles had a banquet of churches, I found the perfect fit—gays and lesbians loving Jesus. Many who attended had received Christ. I listened to the stories of freedom from drugs, the streets. Some had come to this church as a refuge after being thrown out of their family's church.

I was shocked to encounter several former LC members attending the gay church.

The male minister had a husband dying of AIDS. I listened to his story of experiencing the deterioration of his body, knowing he only had a short time to live. He conveyed that he had requested that the Lord give him ten more years and in return he would commit to faithfully share the gospel message with anyone he encountered. The Lord gave him exactly ten years, and when Bea and I arrived on the scene, his funeral would be just a few months later. The pastor shared that his husband would lie on his back, prop the Bible up, and praise Jesus every morning for those he had led to Christ and for the time he had been given. Although some of the testimonies were powerful, I registered extreme compromise.

I was so brokenhearted for Bea that I wanted her to receive Christ. In the midst of darkness, the Gospel still went forth. Every week we attended the services. I loved the worship and some of the preaching, yet I could not ignore the prick in my heart and the true Word of God that never returned void. Although I attended and enjoyed, I never reconciled it. I knew the truth—too much of the truth. I was attempting to name gay and Christian in the same sentence. This was *not* possible for me. It was a contradiction and a lie that they could exist in peace. This quest only furthered spiritual war. God would one day intervene, but in the meantime, this "gay Christian" term was the Enemy's invention in my life.

One afternoon I shared Christ with Bea, and in that moment, she embraced Him. But things would not change with us.

After being together for a year, she took Elizabeth with her to buy me an engagement ring. Bea said if I would make a commitment to marry, she would feel much safer—a rather agonizing request. Yet I did not want to lose her, so I accepted. Gay marriage was not legal, so this was not recognized by the courts. The pastor of the gay church agreed to marry us. The real heartbreak for me was that Bea refused to add Peter and Jim to the guest list. She was jealous of my relationship with them and could not understand why I would have any part of their lives. She came dangerously close in her attempts to cause a complete breach, yet Peter and I had traveled down too many tough roads to let anyone destroy the reconciling work we had done.

Our wedding day arrived, and we launched into a huge fight in the dressing room. I said something wrong, and it sent her into orbit. In my stupor of darkness, I still proceeded down that aisle.

My parents sat in the front row, and I knew my mother was praying. Why did she go? I suspect she inquired of the Lord and received her answer from Him. But this was a dark day for my mother. I saw it in her eyes.

I stood at that altar, taking communion and shaking uncontrollably. The Holy Spirit was so grieved, and the trembling was an outward manifestation. I knew deep inside it was not nerves. I was already encased in Jericho, but more cement, mortar, and bricks were laid that day, and any cracks that allowed the smallest specks of light were sealed with Satan's demonic trowel. The nervous ticks continued throughout the day. I put on a smile and tried to survive.

We went on a honeymoon to Puerto Rico and fought the entire time. At one point I took off my ring and threw it toward the sea. I did retrieve it, but the anger and hurt inside was immense, and this so-called marriage had not solved a thing.

My life played out the powerful verse Ezekiel 16:39: "I shall also give you into the hands of your lovers, and they will tear down your shrines, demolish your high places, strip you of your clothing, take away your jewels, and will leave you naked and bare." In God's unrelenting love for me, He let the tether go a long way, but He never released it.

Bea and I stayed together until 2002. The relationship encompassed violence and swearing and loads of coffee as we sat for hours attempting to resolve the unresolvable. (Yes, lesbians also talk and talk and talk and talk more.) We had no real friends, and we did little with the outside world. Bea resented my attention to Elizabeth. Thankfully, Elizabeth had her dad's home every other week, as Bea and I were two crazy women living under the same roof.

Eventually Bea left without a fight. The insecurities became too much for even her to manage, so she asked me to tell her it was over because she could not do it. By this time, I was done with the drinking and done with the craziness and just wanted peace in my home. It had saddened me to see this young woman crying in bed, clinging to a teddy bear and broken to bits. I understood that pain and never wanted to be another person who rejected her. That had been my biggest trap and the primary reason I stuck in and tried.

That same day I wrote a check and sent her on her way.

It did not take long for me to get back on my feet. About a week later, I went to my normal dry cleaner. The owner was gay, so I got the "family discount." On this particular week, I told her my tale of woe, and she invited me to her birthday party. This party was loaded with gay women, and she promised I would make some new friends. I was all in.

Chapter 12

Partner 2—Keisha

I was excited as I prepped for the party. I had been isolated for five years, so this was like escaping from a cage. Keisha, the owner of the dry cleaner, had a ton of friends, and they all seemed normal. They embraced me with open arms. I had my eye on Keisha though, and I made it known. Keisha had been around the block for considerably more years and was not interested in getting involved, but I was on a mission and eventually succeeded. Three weeks after Bea departed, I went on a date with Keisha. I fell in love, and after six weeks Keisha and I were officially a couple. The circle of gay women friends, both couples and singles, was large, so we went to parties together, and the world enlarged inside Jericho. Yes, it was a bustling city of warmth and "love," but still within a big wall. Soon Keisha sold her home and became part owner of mine.

Keisha was not thin—not obese, but not thin. The first day she met Elizabeth, now ten years old, I served a brunch. We all sat down, and in the course of conversation I said I loved cooking, and Keisha said, "Well, I love to eat."

"I bet you do," Elizabeth said with a darling little smile.

Everyone at the table roared. However, that would not be the last blunt thing Elizabeth would convey to Keisha.

My new love had no belief in God and called herself a borderline atheist. She attended the Church of Religious Science and deemed white witchcraft (Wiccan) as a suitable form of worship. She also had obsessive-compulsive disorder and was not affectionate, and my love language was touch. In addition, she had loads of health issues, so I had to rid the house of garlic and onions, once staples in my home. Keisha had been a senior corporate executive in banking and was now a business owner, so I got dry cleaning for free and did not do laundry.

The first six months, as always, were terrific. That chocolate on the brain and the "new love" experience took over like a predictable drug. But then I started doing things that annoyed her, such as leaving a cotton ball on the sink or accidently using her toothbrush, which was the same color as mine. She took time to write a sticky note rather than throwing the little cotton ball in the trash.

We had some hearty arguments about God, and she was hard as a rock. About two years into our relationship, I embarked on a new career and worked with a believer. He knew I was gay, yet he befriended me and invited me to read the entire Left Behind series, which depicts the rapture and those left behind. They also encapsulated God's redemptive power. I ate those books up as if they were the finest cakes. I purposely bought four at a time so I would never have to wait when I finished one. At lunch breaks, while cooking dinner, and on weekends by the pool, I buried my nose in these books. I used to joke with Keisha that I was going to leave them on the shelf, and if by some chance the Bible was correct, she would have them for ready reference as she navigated her way through the end times. Yet my spirit registered that Jesus better not come too quickly, or I would be navigating with her.

When the last book was published, I sat for sixteen solid hours in my backyard and read it from cover to cover, replaying in my head the part where the Lord came back in the clouds and everyone heard their *own name*. I sat and cried and hoped that someday I would hear Him say, "Cari."

Eventually, Keisha convinced me that I needed mental medication, as my attention deficit disorder was conflicting with her obsessive-compulsive disorder. So like a good soldier, I begged a psychologist to give me a prescription. I knew the buzzwords, and even though the psychologist was a bit perplexed, she had sympathy for my plight. Keisha would leave me if I did not square up and change.

I never took the pills. I made it look like I took the pills. Yet Keisha saw a dramatic change. It wasn't hard to buy a different-color toothbrush or tidy up quick before she got home. I knew how to follow rules from the LC days. I just had to know what the rules were.

Our relationship was not void of trouble, and we decided to go to couples counseling, but the session was Keisha talking, me listening, and the therapist simply nodding her head. Occasionally the therapist would give me this knowing wink, as if she saw right through all the nonsense Keisha dished out.

Keisha encouraged me to go to the therapist on my own, because "I needed more help," and she thought it would accelerate the process. In these private sessions, the therapist challenged me continually to leave Keisha, but I hung in there, hoping improvement was just over the horizon.

Keisha violated some rules that sent *me* over the edge. At twelve years old, Elizabeth had gone to Japan with her cousins and brought back a gift for each of us. The scarf she gave to Keisha, although not exactly her style, was special because of who had given it to Elizabeth. As the gifts were distributed, I could tell Keisha was displeased, and I could not imagine such ungratefulness. I probed the subject the next morning, and Keisha threw the scarf on the top shelf and said, "It's not my style."

I popped like a roaring lion, and I slugged her with all my might. It was as if she had thrown Elizabeth on the shelf, and that was beyond intolerable. She could beat me into the ground with her OCD, but this tapped an anger that sent me over the edge. This was a very painful time on many levels, as I also worried about myself.

During our relationship, I met a seventy-year-old woman at a car repair shop. While engaged in casual conversation, she told me about her African safari, and her animation, energy, and passion captivated me.

I decided to go on a safari to Africa on my own to clear my head. It had been a dream of mine, and I was driven to seize the day. Given Keisha's stomach issues, such a trip for her was out of the question, and I was grateful. Keisha and Elizabeth stayed alone together while I traveled for seventeen days. I embraced primitive tent camping, bungee jumping three hundred feet over Victoria Falls, and the company of hyenas at suppertime.

While I vacationed, though, Keisha seized an opportunity to pour her deep lies into Elizabeth's vulnerable heart.

When I returned, Elizabeth came in our room at night, wanting to sleep in our bed because she was scared. I thought this highly unusual and questioned it often. Elizabeth would simply say that she had fears in the night. Finally we figured out that putting a sleeping bag by our bed was a better solution so we would not all be awakened.

I discovered years later, much to my horror, that crazy Keisha had told Elizabeth that I did not love her and might kill her in the night. She came in the room so that Keisha would protect her. This was by far the sickest thing I had ever heard and believe it to be straight from the pit of hell. I was glad Elizabeth had the courage to share so we could continue our healing process. Sin is relentless and damaging, and this was clearly a large ravage.

Life with Keisha had another hook of bondage. She was half owner of the home. Although I was miserable, I knew if we parted ways, it would be financial ruin. On Christmas day 2004, Keisha proposed marriage, much to my astonishment. She was the last person I wanted to marry. I wanted her gone, but I did not want to lose everything. I put on a smile and said yes. At that time, domestic partnerships were in full swing. Additionally, Keisha wanted to buy a business with the equity in the home. I was not in favor of this proposition, but she was considerably stronger willed than I, and I dwelled in fear much of the time.

Elizabeth was in her early teens and a bit mouthy. She tested the limits on every level. Public high school in Los Angeles was not an option. So we enrolled her in parochial school. We used to jokingly say that Elizabeth attended school six days a week instead of five. The nuns at her Catholic school appreciated her well-rounded social skills, but they were dismayed by the inappropriate nouns and verbs that she deliberately threw into her sentences. She embraced shock value in her highly intelligent and calculated manner, always with a cheeky smile. As a result, Elizabeth had her own Saturday morning breakfast club of a rebellious yet lovable bunch of feisty boys and girls. Peter and I had instilled a high level of confidence and independent thinking, and it was clear that we had done an excellent job! In spite of my poor example, Elizabeth had her voice.

She hated watching how I so readily adapted to being controlled, and she resented that I did not stand up for myself. She was also angry with me for putting so much else first. Some of her acting out was dangerous, yet God also spared Elizabeth from serious consequences. (Years later I would have to face the impact and deal with the ramifications before the Lord and repent of deplorable parenting.)

One day, Keisha and I fought over my mothering skills. Elizabeth sat at the table, and Keisha got in her face and made a demand. Elizabeth lifted her finger, got right in Keisha's face, and said, "You are not my mom, you will never be my mom, and you will never have authority over what I do."

Keisha left the table. Elizabeth looked at me, and it did not take a rocket scientist to know the end of my relationship with Keisha was near. That might not seem like a God moment, but it was. The hutzpah that Elizabeth possessed and exhibited was another demonstration of the amazing grace of God in protecting me from a tragedy that would have lifelong consequences.

Keisha packed her bags and broke off the engagement. I was not upset, but I was terrified of losing my home and having no place for Elizabeth. By all rights Keisha deserved half, as she had sold her home and moved into mine. But Keisha was one smart lady and had been through this before, so she knew exactly how to psychologically spin my head and get what she wanted. Peter picked up Elizabeth, as the rest of the day was nothing short of hellish.

The unexpected grace that my parents displayed through this crisis was undeserved. I had made my bed with my disastrous choices, and if I lost my home, I deserved it. Keisha had offered to let me pull out a loan with interest to pay her back as long as I did it within four years. This would have meant being linked to her for all that time. My mom approached me about reverse mortgaging my grandparents' home. My biological uncle lived in the home and was not well, and a reverse mortgage would secure more than enough to pay Keisha her due. My dear parents bailed me out even though I deserved to be smashed like a bug. The last thing my mother wanted was for me to be tied to Keisha. This was a shining example of unmerited favor, one I didn't take for granted.

Much transpired as Keisha and I split belongings and figured out the finances, but in the end, through my parents' gracious gift, I wrote Keisha a check in exchange for her signing over the deed to the house. That night I cooked a dinner filled with garlic and onions! Elizabeth and I celebrated. It was unfortunate that I had to do laundry and ironing, but I adjusted quickly to my freedom.

After partner two, poetry emerged, quiet and still even though my struggle was deep. I wrote "Lost" by the fire one night.

LOST

My sacred sanctuary where I meditate
Yet scenery has changed and I can't relate.
Lost in familiar, now just a guest
In loneliness pine, my chair I detest.
I shut my eyes and life starts to spin
I brace for control but know I won't win.

Handles I seek melt into the walls

And those in the future I beckon and call.

Music so foreign, the words never heard

And as the lights dim, toward darkness I'm lured.

Cushions and rugs turn into cement

And legs that did balance are folded and bent.

Pictures with forms become just abstract color

And a wall has erected where once was a door.

Frozen in time, but this dance in the fire

An image of harmony, yet peace not acquired.

My eyes are transfixed yet my body can't move

As I'm led to the place where my soul can be soothed.

This present, the now, all anxiety dispersed

It can't be predicted and never rehearsed.

The room slows its pace to a steady-state zone

My heart fills with light. I stand—I am home!

The Online Quest

In 2005 online dating started to get legs. We were all victims of AOL dial-up, so the lack of internet speed was taxing. I could not stand the prospect of being alone. I needed someone in my life all the time. As I trolled the internet, I found a variety of lesbians. I was not particularly drawn to the overly masculine or heavily tattooed type, but I dated a wide array. One in particular had a dog she loved to such a degree that it accompanied us on every date. The dog was large and drooled in hefty amounts. While dining at a nice steak house, the dog lay under the table, licking my shoe and cleaning his mouth on my black dress pants. I sat there and did not say a word, but that was our last date.

Lesbian dating sites were no different from the regular ones. Pictures hardly ever represented the person, and the visual was high on my list. If the photo showed a thin beauty, I was ill prepared for who actually showed up. I did not appreciate the deceit or being called superficial. I was a bit too deep for most, as I broached the God question. I also had a bad habit of elevating a positive quality to such a massive degree that the disastrous ones took a backseat, at least for a few weeks.

I was fascinated by the number of married women, supposedly straight women, who posted online *seeking women*. I had a less-than-favorable opinion about these women and knew they were playing with a hot poker stick with a gasoline tip, waving it through the fires of hell and believing they would not get burned.

One single gal in my online adventures, though, captured my attention for two months. We spoke on the phone for hours on end and fell in love before even meeting face to face. Our whirlwind romance lasted over a Christmas season when she came to visit me. After her departure, I believed I could not live even a day without her, so I flew to her. The morning after my arrival, she abruptly said she could not go on, told me to pack, and took me to the airport. This was in Kansas City, Missouri, and the next flight to Los Angeles was ten hours later. I sat there heartbroken and in utter disbelief, waiting for a flight, but God met me. I did not deserve for Him to enter the scene, but He saw me and had compassion. He knew my heart. He knew my longings.

I took some aspirin before boarding the plane. Exhausted, I closed my eyes and asked God to heal my heart. Within a few days, I was back to normal and back in the saddle again on my quest for the one who would satisfy.

One day I landed on a picture that captivated me. Leslie. She lived in another state and had a daughter as well. We spoke on the phone and hit it off instantly. The common scenes of our lives contained uncanny similarities: ways in which we perceived the world, engaged our senses, and even related to God. Over the course of a few weeks, we planned a trip to meet face to face. Then out of the blue, Leslie had her one and only business trip. And our meeting was off. When I probed for another date, Leslie thought I might be neurotic. Brokenhearted, I wrote her a long letter. A number of months later, we reconnected by phone, but by that time we had both entered into a relationship (my third partner).

Leslie and I communicated on and off for a number of years. We seemed to finish each other's sentences and shared songs over the wires. I sent Leslie many letters and poetry, and many times I wondered if someday, when our children were grown, I would end up with her as the love of my life.

Through my struggles, I prayed a critical prayer with tears over and over again: *God, will you do for me what I cannot do for myself?* I didn't necessarily know what I was praying or asking for. I just knew that the pain in my life was becoming unbearable. I'd faced moments of utter despair in my relationships. I just wanted to be loved. *Why wouldn't they just love me?* I would sit at the foot of the bed, weeping as if I were about to take my last breath, crying out for the pain to go away. Bea would shut down, and Keisha would mock and run away. The third and final long-term, Rhoda, denied physical affection to get her way. Sometimes I would lie curled up in a fetal position, wondering how in the world I got here and wondering if I would ever escape. I suspect Rahab in Jericho had the same experience. As she lay with men who couldn't care less about her, she probably cried and wondered if the God of Israel had the slightest concern.

My prayer was the groaning of the Holy Spirit inside me. I had no idea what I wanted or needed. I simply knew I was trapped. By now the walls were so high and the mortar so thick that I could barely hear God. I had stopped attending the gay church because of Keisha. My language had become akin to that of a truck driver, and the callouses around my heart grew like an invasive mold. The beast that wanted to be fed was never satisfied. Yet there were moments in my ninety-minute car ride to work that I was mesmerized by the sunrise and traveled to my happy place. This particular poem was one of the outcomes. I find it fascinating that every poem I have ever written ends on a redemptive note even though I felt far from redeemed.

In the midst of my own subconscious internal horror of psychological entrapment and slavery, I wrote this poem on the back of checkbook stubs, as I had no paper in my car.

BROKEN

This hole in my heart where threads were unwoven
Rays of hope spewing out as all light was so stolen.
They tugged on the strands unraveling more
Blood pumped with fury to settle the score.
My skin became pale yet bruises burst forth
Shocked by the contrast, those wounds of my worth.
Bathing in pools to wash my rejection
Yet murky and stagnant replaced my reflection.
Hands lost their grasp and feet lost sensation
Crippled and weary, no self-realization.
They teased with some mending, the one who had ravaged
Their needles then pierced and furthered the damage.
This destitute state now dependent at best
As they smothered out life and I heaved from my chest.
Pleading for breath from this one so adored
Yet blank words of care and eyes filled with scorn.
My friends were all gone, only watched from afar
They tried to talk sense but saw all my scars.
My body was drained; will this nightmare continue?
Yet my soul had its voice and so craved a new venue.
It spoke words of freedom and wove threads of love
And reminded of those with a view from above.

Hole sealed in my heart, circulation returned
It was not just my pain but to share what I learned.
Then hours were days, then months, then a year
Fog now has lifted. I stand tall in the clear!

During my online internet travels, one gal asked me to "describe my higher power." Such a strange question, but I pondered in quiet for a few days, and I created this next poem. What was written was contrary to my experience at this juncture. There are bits that could be assigned to other moments of my past. Still, this represents someone who has come home to the Lord. My, how God truly does see the end from the beginning. The Holy Spirit's birthing of this poem is commensurate with that truth. It did not come from the fleshly me, as I was doing it my way when I wrote it.

MY HIGHER POWER

Since the day you were young and made a decision
Your life *My* design with such perfect precision.
When you thought you'd lost strength and were just short of beaten
I restored years that the locust had eaten.
When you cried on your pillow pleading *I'd* hear
I responded with warmth and saved every tear.
When you wandered with mission and selfishly roamed
I was the one propelling you home.
When you screamed and you cursed and launched like a stallion
I took the reins to calm your rebellion.
When sorrow and pain of relationships ended
From your knees to your feet, you stood, your heart mended.
When peace was your hope but you lived in dissention
You closed your eyes and got *My* attention.
When you were so pressed and then poised for debate

I stopped your tongue—"Allow *Me* to relate."
When you pursued things that you thought were your wish
I guarded in quiet so *My* will you wouldn't miss.
When you thought you could manage and you knew best
I was there when you tired and *My* grace was your rest.
The literature of life you have reached out to grasp
Yet *My* timing is perfect so inscriptions will last.
Nothing is random, all those dreams in your head
I know your soul and have woven the threads.
Let your heart open wide to paths so uncharted
Don't stop dreaming big, the Red Sea *I* parted.
Expect that *I* know the rooms of your soul
They are integral to what makes you whole.
And where you feel blanks let *Me* fill in the spaces
As love will reflect in all of *My* faces.

Chapter 13

Partner 3—Rhoda

In view of the online disasters, I altered my selection criteria. Tired of women who had never been a parent and were unable to embrace Elizabeth, I decided pursuing another mother would be best. This narrowed the field considerably, but in early 2006, I met Rhoda. Rhoda had three beautiful daughters, and it was love at first sight.

Rhoda was up front about her debt. In my quest for love, I paid off thousands of dollars of debts and cleared all her income tax and credit card bills within the first two months. I couldn't blame her, because she didn't ask. I did it to "free her." What I didn't realize was that I was literally and figuratively mirroring Ezekiel 16:34: "You give money and no money is given to you." I was paying all of my lovers!

Rhoda also had her share of history and read just about every New Age book. She attended a women's group and their "house of healing" in Washington, DC. She couldn't work much because of back issues, so I offered to fund the tab for her monthly treks across the country. She believed in God but wanted no part of Jesus. I was OK with that. It was all relative, and she was a clear step up from Keisha. Though kind and gracious to Elizabeth, Rhoda was jealous because Elizabeth had three working parents (Peter, Jim, and me) funding her life, while Rhoda was a single mom to three grown daughters. This ratio unsettled her greatly and led to continual stress in our relationship.

Eckhart Tolle's *Power of Now and A New Earth* had flooded bookstores, and we participated in the global online webinar orchestrated by the Oprah show. It sounded good, and to my clouded ears bordered on biblical. Clearly the Enemy had packaged a counterfeit god in this New Age bow wave.

After returning from one of her weekends to Washington, DC, Rhoda told me about sweathouses, being blindfolded for hours, and how some of the people would go into trances and start chanting like animals. This raised a caution flag and prompted me to do some serious research. I had seen this firsthand in other settings while married to Peter and was keenly familiar with occult practices. After digging deep, I uncovered that one of the leaders of this healing house was part of an African demonic group that worshiped multiple gods. I knew I could not fund such evil. In spite of the dark place I was walking, the Lord rose up in me, and I spent two days sharing with Rhoda the dangers of the occult and the diabolical source of this women's group. I reneged on my promise to pay subsequent tuition and monthly visits. She had to choose: Washington, DC, or me.

Since I was a large part of her support, the decision was not hard. But she resented it in the years to follow, as these people had become her friends. Based on my experience in the LC, I could understand and appreciate the impact. But her exit from this DC group was a huge protection for both of us. Rhoda would have been destroyed, and there would have been an even darker influence on our home.

Since Rhoda believed in God, we went to the gay church I had attended a few years earlier. I was glad to return, as it represented some semblance of connection. Rhoda meditated every morning with a slug of New Age books. (Some years later in my own devotion, I landed on Ecclesiastes 12:12: Be warned: the writing of many books is endless, and excessive devotion to books is wearying to the body. I thought, *Ha, even the Bible had something to say about it.* Rhoda always questioned why I would not quiet myself and meditate.

"Well, somebody has to work" was my flippant comment. In reality, I had no appetite for the Word. Whenever I briefly considered the matter of spending time in the Bible, I went back to 5:30 a.m. force-fed morning watches and decided it was not for me. The Word already convicted me daily, so I wasn't about to read it and intensify the heat. I had to shut off the Holy Spirit's speaking in order to stay sane. Even in the gay church, while everyone seemed at peace, I could not reconcile that God was OK with everything. Sometimes I would pray a simple prayer: *God, can you please delay your return so that I do not have to spend one thousand years in outer darkness?* I was pretty sure that one thousand years in darkness would get me to my knees, but I had already experienced a seven-year prison in the LC, so the idea of one thousand years sent chills down my spine, and I never got so cocky to think that God changed His mind about sin.

At the beginning of our relationship, Rhoda made me promise that we would move out of Los Angeles to somewhere east. I would have promised anything just to keep the relationship. Little did I know that God had something in mind.

Elizabeth was in her midteens, and although she enjoyed having sisters who visited regularly, the level of heated estrogen in our home was becoming too much to bear. In addition, I was not a stellar mom by any standard, and she and I would yell and scream. She had no sense of constancy in my home. Peter and Jim had been together steadily, so by all rights, their home represented far more stability than the mess I provided. Elizabeth had been in therapy, and one fated day she said she did not want to live with me anymore.

On one hand I was relieved, because I could not handle my own inner tragedy, yet I also knew I had failed greatly as a mother and broken the promise I had made to her time and time again— "You and I will change the world." I willingly allowed her to live with Peter and Jim full time. I had nothing left inside and did not want Elizabeth to be a victim of my depleted state. This was a hard-to-numb pain.

Resentment built between Rhoda and me, as everything was about equality. If Elizabeth got money, then I was expected to give her three grown daughters the equivalent. The affordability factor with me as the sole income provider made this an impossible feat, and it drained me daily. (Her daughters and I were close though, and I am happy one of them surrendered her life to God and is now clean and sober. I was privileged to be a witness of this just recently and was thrilled by the transformation.)

Elizabeth was in her senior year, and the promise I made to Rhoda about moving was about to come to pass. In August of 2008, I traveled to the United Kingdom on business, and my boss approached me about a position in Twinsburg, Ohio. I stared at him and thought he was joking. Who would want to move to northeast Ohio? Maybe the Carolinas, but Ohio? He smiled and asked me to think about it. On my twelve-hour direct flight home, the Lord Jesus Christ showed up on that plane. It was as if He sat next to me, speaking into my mind and heart as I pondered and went in and out of dozing and sleeping. By the time I landed in Los Angeles, I was excited about the prospect. When I spoke to Rhoda about it, she was pleased because her father and stepmother lived in Concord, Ohio. Maybe a new venue would fix everything? I interviewed for the position and was shocked when I didn't get it. I couldn't understand why God had placed a desire in my heart for Ohio since it wasn't going to happen. So I let it go.

In October that same year, my boss asked me fly to Ohio the next day to interview for a management position. The timing of the transfer was more suitable, because I had completed the setup of a new division of the company such that it could be transitioned to North Carolina and combined with another team. My heart leaped, as the new position included a promotion and all relocation expenses.

I flew to Cleveland the first week in October, interviewed for the position in Twinsburg, and was offered the job the next day. The largest quandary was that Elizabeth was in her senior year in high school and would not be part of the move, and I felt I was abandoning her. That was tough, but deep inside I knew I needed to leave Los Angeles.

Rhoda and I had finished remodeling the inside of our home, so it was sale ready. My real estate agent listed it a few days later and sold the house in seventeen hours in a depressed market, above list price. We looked online and eyed a home in Hudson, Ohio. By the second week of October, I was in the Realtor's office in Hudson, signing the papers for that home. While in the office, my buyers called and asked if they could close in fifteen days. If I agreed, they would waive all inspections. This was unheard of in Los Angeles. The Realtor and I shook hands, and I said, "We can do this."

Rhoda and I flew home, and in a race against time, I sold items, put things out at the curb, and distributed to friends and family. I barely had time to say goodbye to anyone. I had no time to think. Much of the move was a blur. However, God enveloped my fear of leaving Elizabeth and my hometown to relocate to a place where everything would be unknown. The movers came in, packed everything up, and drove off. Our cars were picked up a few days later, and we met the movers in northeast Ohio.

I still walked in deep darkness, yet I was financially blessed above and beyond and was gifted with the most beautiful home. The expanse of the yard, the greenery, the colors, the space—I could not believe I lived here. My yard reflected the happy place I had traveled to in my mind over the years. This was another picture of undeserved grace.

All the space in the home, including the countertops, was filled with Rhoda's trinkets. Many of her items had been in storage in Los Angeles, but now that we had triple the space, we had room for triple the stuff. I could only stand three things max on a tabletop. If the table was small, the three things better be small. Anything more and my world felt crowded, and I could not breathe. One night I came home to miniature houses going down the stairway. I hyperventilated and yelled, "These have to go *now!*" Rhoda resentfully removed them and placed them in one of many boxes.

Shortly after moving to Ohio, I ate lunch at the Panera Bread in Hudson on a Sunday afternoon. Seated at the tables was the after-church crowd, so some ladies were discussing the sermon. For some odd reason, and because I was not shy, I asked if they were Christians. One lady gave me her phone number and shared about a church close by. I tucked it away.

A few weeks later, Rhoda and I decided to try some churches. She was on a mission to try all of them, and based on my count in Hudson alone, I anticipated a long journey. Our first stop was a traditional place. It was pleasant, but I got wind of a big scandal by accidently overhearing a dialogue and decided there was too much drama. That was the last thing I needed.

The following week I called the lady from Panera and asked directly, "Does your church accept gay people?"

Without sounding critical, she said what many Christians say, "We love the sinner but not the sin."

For a person who identified as gay, this was absolutely the wrong thing to say, because gay was me. We were not two separate entities. I was not necessarily desiring an answer that was completely welcoming. I just wanted simplicity: "Cari, our church loves Jesus, and we would be delighted for you to come and see." That response would have diffused my rapid-fire reaction of emphatically expressing I had *no* intention of attending. Sometimes direct questions are best not answered directly.

A few days later, as Rhoda and I drove around town, she spotted a church—the same church I had recently discussed with the Panera lady. I could not deny Rhoda's request to see it because of my desire for her to become a believer. It was a Saturday morning, so we drove in the parking lot and proceeded to the lobby. I was antsy and told the receptionist that I liked to sleep in late on Sundays and the services were probably too early. That was a miserable failure because this church held services almost every hour—ugh.

So the next day, there we sat in the third-row center at the late service. I loved the worship, and I knew many of the songs.

That first Sunday, we sat next to a woman named Brigette. She became one of the first prayer warriors in Ohio to pray for us. We met a number of other people on that visit, and I did not care whether they accepted us or not. I liked the place, and I intended to stay. The resemblance of the pastor to my dad was uncanny. It was no wonder that my subconscious mind registered this church as familiar. I felt at home. What a wonderful and detailed God wink.

Rhoda and I were open about our relationship when folks at the church would inquire. When I said, "Oh, she is my partner," they would usually ask, "What kind of business?" And I would say, "Life, a life partner." No one raised their eyebrows or made a face. I was convinced God led us to the people we were designed to meet.

Rhoda was still on a quest to try all the churches, but I was done and thought it a waste of time to check out any more.

Oh, if that gal in Panera had known how God had worked.

Our church attendance was up and down because we spent Sunday mornings rehashing the fight we'd had the night before. Also, we were unprepared for winter weather. I had one jacket to my name and no winter clothes, and shopping consumed many weekends.

When spring neared, we joined a country club, a luxury we couldn't have afforded in California. In Hudson the monthly rate was dirt cheap. Golf season hit in early spring, and I learned how to play with the kind of golf clubs that included a bag when purchased at a sporting goods store. I owned only one pair of golf shoes, but that didn't matter. I loved the game and made friends.

Rhoda rarely came to the club, which frustrated me because I wanted a social life. Needless to say, she became a golf widow.

We became more known in the church, and some members also frequented the country club. Rhoda did not desire more friends, while I, on the other hand, wanted friends, so I convinced her to join the church's mentor program. We showed up on a Wednesday night, and as I scanned the room, I thought, *Well, my odds are pretty good of getting a fun pal and maybe even a golf buddy.* We wrote our brief autobiographies, and I was honest about my identity struggle, burying a subtle cry for help between the handwritten lines. Rhoda went the religious route and wrote how she desired deep knowledge of the Bible and growth in Christ.

Later at home I said, "Why did you write such craziness, 'grow in Christ'? You don't even know Him!" That night as I lay in bed, the Lord spoke to my heart. *Cari, will you embrace whomever I provide?* This question indicated I would not get a little golf buddy as my mentor.

The ladies' leadership deemed me a bit of a tough case, so they went outside the bounds and called on someone who had not even attended the previous Wednesday—Mary Jane.

I received my name tag and walked with anticipation into the next room to find my mentor. There she was. Not what I had in mind as a *social* replacement for my miserable relationship with Rhoda, but she was exactly what God had in mind. I chuckled inside, since the Lord had prepared me the night before. As we sat eye to eye at the table, I perceived Mary Jane's quandary, because she had never met a gay person. I had made a commitment to meet weekly, so I intended to see it through.

Rhoda was excited about her mentor, as they were about the same age.

My first meeting with Mary Jane comprised a simple cup of coffee and light conversation. I did not want a study, and I did not want the Bible. Mary Jane must have discerned this, because she never pressed me for either.

Rhoda met her mentor the same day, and that night we compared notes. Rhoda's homework encompassed reading the book of

John in conjunction with a meaty dissertation on the backdrop of John's writings. This was no fault of her mentor. Rhoda had asked for this in her embellished autobiography. I laughed almost to the point of tears as I proudly said, "My mentor and I just sat and had coffee."

The third week I met with Mary Jane, we wandered around a park and sat on a little bench. She asked what it was like to be gay. Her eyes had such love in them, and I knew she truly wanted to know. She was not out to fix or correct my behavior—she just wanted a better understanding. My heart opened wide. I shared my struggles with gut-wrenching honesty, and I cried. This represented a turning point in our relationship, because I trusted her, and I knew she was for me, not against me. Mary Jane was not on some urgent mission. She was simply being faithful to the Lord and to a calling that led her outside her comfort zone. God saw her in my life before the foundation of the world, and in His infinite wisdom and timing, moved heaven and earth to establish this encounter. He also prepared my heart to be open—it was *all* Him.

Over the next few months, we never cracked open the Bible or did a study. Rhoda, on the other hand, had a much different experience. She reaped the benefits of fibbing. Many in the church deemed Rhoda as the one who would eventually turn her heart. She had the softer look and seemed more open to the Word. Appearances were deceiving though, as the outward packages were scrutinized and others started writing her next life chapter. Only God knew our hearts though. Only God saw the tears that fell on my pillow at night. Only God knew the impact of sin and brokenness, and only God knew exactly what He would accomplish to display His amazing glory and grace in His perfect time.

I had an image to protect. The shell around my soul had a multitude of fractures. If I allowed someone to press too hard, it might be the final straw and yield a catastrophic shatter. In spite of this, I let Mary Jane in because of her gentleness and kindness. She was not out to fix. She simply pointed me to Christ in subtle ways.

Most of the time I barely noticed. This was a similar experience to my sponsor in Al-Anon. Both knew that it was the Lord's work, not theirs, and neither let ego or pride enter the scene.

Life in Ohio evolved in a positive way. I enjoyed golfing, and I had more friends than I ever had in Los Angeles, since all the bridges to my young past had been obliterated in the LC. I adored my new church in Ohio. But I was still trapped in my own Jericho. On the surface my life seemed good, but my relationship with Rhoda spiraled downward. Bitterness and resentment grew like an invasive mold. Money equality remained a hot topic. I was frustrated because we couldn't move forward and connect after a fight. I did not understand why the anger had to linger for days, even weeks. I resented that she could sleep in while I had to get up early for work. In reality, she was no longer satisfying, as nothing but Christ could fill the void. Ohio had not altered anything, and I plunged into depression—even a new environment and a beautiful home did not hold the secret ingredient to joy and happiness.

The Sermon

In September 2009, after Mary Jane and I had been meeting for approximately five months, the pastor shared a message on Galatians 5:19: "Now the deeds of the flesh are evident, which are: immorality, impurity, sensuality." It was the first time he unequivocally named homosexuality in the context of sexual deviance. He spoke confidently that it was contrary to God's design for our lives. This was a word delivered in an uncompromising way and bolstered the Word in a manner pleasing to the Lord. He spoke boldly, and I was grateful, as compromise from the pulpit might have been the greatest enemy to the Lord's transforming work in my own life. Rhoda and I sat in our normal third-row seats. Many loving eyes gazed upon us, and I later discovered that silent prayers burst forth for both of us during that message.

My response was a quiet one. I already knew the truth in the Word and had "successfully" avoided its impact on numerous occasions. Yet somehow this struck a different chord. A large part of my openness was the pastor's physical similarity to my father, such that the delivery was not coming from merely a minister. It was being spoken by the earthly father I had longed for my whole life, one who would courageously speak wisdom into my life and protect me from deep harm. What a testament to God. He moved heaven and earth to have a man be my pastor who looked just like my own dad. What undeniable divine detail.

Rhoda was madder than a wet hen and thought we were absolute idiots for continuing to attend a church that thought our relationship was sexually deviant. In the logical realm, I couldn't argue her position, but I was still drawn. I had been tethered to Him from the time I was five and a half. So even though I thought I was in charge, that tether would only allow me to go so far. That day I felt the tug of the tether, but I lacked the capacity to respond. I just knew this church was home, and I was not about to leave despite any opinions in the church about our relationship.

Sweet Mary Jane called to ask how I was doing. I made sure to present confident Cari and simply responded that I already knew how the church felt and that it was no surprise and had no effect. For the next few days I surveyed the wall to make sure everything was intact. *Looking good*, I thought. What I did not see were the prayer warriors—my mother included—marching outside and around my wall of Jericho in silence.

* * *

Joshua 6:10 says, "But Joshua commanded the people [before they started to march], saying, 'You shall not shout nor let your voice be heard nor let a word proceed out of your mouth, until the day I tell you, "Shout!" Then you shall shout!'" The premise of silence jumps out in this Scripture. For those unfamiliar with the story, prior to the walls of Jericho tumbling, the children of Israel were charged to march around the wall in silence for days until it was God's time for them to shout. Imagine that—complete silence for days, and they did not know how many days they would have to do this. It ended up being six, and on the seventh, the shout. I have pondered this truth in my own prayer life. God does not give us the time period—He just says to march in silent prayer until He says otherwise. We think we have to beat the wall, scream at the wall, or yell at the people inside the wall. Yet God said, "March." (I suspect the Israelites did much internal praying during those six days of silence.) That wall stood between the Israelites and the good land. Additionally, there was a woman named Rahab, who was the apple of God's eye, trapped inside biblical Jericho, and God had ordained her freedom before the foundation of the world. God had foreordained my freedom, and He established many marchers.

Mary Jane subsequently asked if I wanted to meet the pastor in person. *What a strange question*, I thought. This man just delivered a message and called my life sin. Why in the world would I go back for more? But I agreed. Only God could move in such a way. I never told Rhoda I was going, and in hindsight, that was a wise decision.

Mary Jane accompanied me to the pastor's office. The minute I walked in I said, "I'm not sure why I am here, but I'm gay, and you are not going to convince me otherwise. By the same token, I don't expect to be able to change your mind either." I made sure the stage was set and that the guards around my wall held their positions with guns ready to fire. I was correct in that statement, as man would not be able to change me, and I certainly was not going to be able to change God.

His response was intriguing and a surprise. "I'm glad you are here, because I have always wanted a gay friend."

Wow, calling me *friend!* God used that one sentence to open my heart, and I poured out my life through tears. In the end, I looked right into the pastor's eyes and said, "Do you believe I am saved?"

"Yes, I believe you are saved. However, I do not believe you are living in God's best for your life. Celibacy would be the best thing."

My love language was touch. I laughed and said, "You try that for a month and tell me if it works for you." I could not imagine such a crazy thing. Even though Rhoda had denied me in this arena, I still had hope that one day we would return to normal.

The pastor requested that I keep coming to the church but made it clear that membership was not possible, which suited me just fine. At the end, he said he would pray for me. I made him promise that he would *not* pray that I would stop being gay. I did not ask what he would pray, but at least he made a commitment that he would not pray for a sweeping clean.

I knew what Luke 11:24–26 said: "When the unclean spirit has gone out of a man, it passes through waterless places seeking rest, and not finding any, it says, 'I will return to my house from which I came.' And when it comes, it finds it swept and put in order. Then it goes and takes along seven other spirits more evil than itself, and they go in and live there. And the last state of that man becomes worse than the first." The mere thought that he or anyone else might pray for homosexuality to depart terrified me. I could barely handle my current entrapment. The possibility of life becoming seven times worse was a plight I would not wish on my worst enemy.

Ironically, I enjoyed the meeting with the pastor and was no worse for the wear. It seemed innocuous and casual, and we were both free to share our hearts. All was well.

Depravity and Despair

In the two months following that meeting, darkness hit my soul like never before. Anger and hate seized me like a noose. I examined my dim and lifeless eyes in the mirror and thought I was aging at an accelerated pace. Joy, the infrequent guest, had packed its bags and left. I still met with Mary Jane, but I had little to say. The dialogue focused on disgust with my relationship and the need to move on. I thought a trip might fix things, so I planned one for Rhoda and me Thanksgiving weekend. My language had accelerated to a new level of profanity, and the walls of Jericho closed in like a vice on my soul. I even stopped praying *God, will you do for me what I cannot do for myself?* All strength had gone, yet my world of work, golf, and church continued like a moving sidewalk. Life was marching forward, but I was ceasing to exist. I barely listened to the sermons. The shell with its thin fractures broke apart. I looked in the mirror and screamed, "I hate you!"

By the world's standards, I had it all. In reality, I had lost Elizabeth, I could not hear even a tiny voice of God, and death was not an option because I was so frightened of those one thousand years. Evil and Light were battling inside—a war like none other. Yet the depravity led to composition.

THE CONTRAST

Evil sits in the dark and lies there in wait
It screams of confusion with noise of debate.
Light is the calm with such a small voice
It strokes our hearts gently so we make the choice.
Evil tugs at our brains and threatens such loss
It paints on the surface perceptions of cost.
Light cuddles our souls and guides to our rest
Shows an entrance of peace, but faith is the test.
Evil nags with such logic and numbs all our pain
It tricks us to think that its path is true gain.
Light takes our hands and walks with our hurt
And when danger threatens it keeps us alert.
Evil cuts at our weakness and shames us to action
It dresses in finery to invoke such attraction.

Light covers the vulnerable with a blanket of grace

There is nothing pretentious in that holy place.

Evil skips on deep slopes to achieve the divine

Yet each time it falters, it erects a false shrine.

The Light's hills and valleys embrace all that are mortal

The simple and human who know Truth as the portal.

Evil the source of such dark deprivation

And those sleepless nights with waves of frustration.

Yet Light serves the meals that nourish the soul

Light wakes us from slumber—its love makes us whole.

Evil had consumed me, and Satan was laughing. He and the hellish demons thought their win was just over the horizon. Why wouldn't they? Apparently, all the battles had been seemingly theirs up to this point, as they had Cari encased in the place where no one could get in and no one could go out. Their tailor-made Jericho. Yet those wicked spirits also saw the people marching, marching, marching. My mother and close friends formed the initial small gathering, but God's handpicked, modern-day, consecrated children of Israel increased by the day, and the powers of hell trembled at the prospect that the living God might just bust down that wall. They had witnessed it before with Rahab.

In early November that year, as I drove through Peninsula, Ohio, I stopped the car and called Leslie, the woman I had never met in person but with whom I had a symbiotic and vibrant relationship. I declared my love through tears and asked her to wait, because I had finally decided to leave Rhoda so Leslie and I could live happily ever after.

It was a brave call because I had never been this direct with Leslie, who was on board and had waited for this for several years. Surely this would bring peace and joy.

Chapter 14

Freedom

I had not made the exit from Rhoda yet, as I faced many complexities in parting ways with her. It had to be gradual and deliberate, as we were enmeshed. Rhoda had always wanted to see the Poconos, and I thought a vacation might change things, even though I had my long-term sights set on Leslie. On November 23, 2009, just a couple of days before the vacation, I entered the office in my home and sat on the couch. The circumstances prior to this were a blur. I could not describe any event that had landed me in this room. What I knew was that a place inside me was ready to listen. The lack of speaking from the Lord, His silence, had almost killed me the previous couple of months after my visit with the pastor. On occasion I would still hear Him, so at least I knew He was there. But the recent two-month silence was deafening.

I sat on the couch, folded my hands, and simply said, "Lord, if you have something to say, this is your one chance to say it, and I will listen." Since I knew He spoke through His Word, I grabbed my Bible off the high shelf. Then I proceeded with a step a Christian is guided never to do: randomly open a Bible, plop a finger down, and see what the Lord has to say.

I took the Bible in hand, closed my eyes, and said, "God, please speak to me. Don't ignore me any longer." When I looked down, my finger landed on Luke 3:4–6:

> As it is written in the book of the words of Isaiah the prophet, "The voice of one crying in the wilderness, make ready the way of the Lord, make His paths straight. Every

ravine shall be filled, and every mountain and hill shall be brought low; and the crooked will become straight, and the rough roads smooth; and all flesh shall see the salvation of God."

I simply responded, "OK," and at that moment the living God reached into the deepest place inside and said, *You don't need this anymore. I am enough.* I knew in an instant He had healed me. The hole in my soul no longer existed. It seemed as if He had been sewing His thread of redemption and love alongside that fallen DNA thread that had weaved its way through every part of my being. This day He removed it! He was not in the business of just sweeping my "house" clean. His mission was to fill my "house" with Himself.

I went into spiritual shock. He changed me! This was the end of my homosexual struggle and the end of my homosexual life. It felt like a divine bomb had exploded inside me. One touch by God and *my walls of Jericho came tumbling down.* I experienced the light, deep love of God and the power of God. He filled the hole of fallen desire for the creature and replaced it with Himself. No human words could convey what happened in that minute from 7:01 p.m. to 7:02 p.m. God had answered my simple prayer that I had uttered for years through tears, heartache, and pain: *God, will you do for me what I cannot do for myself?* In His kindness, He responded. He always knew He would, but now it was my reality on earth. Other than that little word *OK*, I was completely speechless. In a minute my entire world structure and vantage point had altered. The walls no longer stood between me and the good land of His divine purpose for my life. He set me free. The darkness and shadows were overcome by saturating light.

I do not remember leaving the room or going to bed that night. Rhoda was away and not expected to return until the next evening. I lay alone in that God-ordained moment in time, and I simply fell asleep.

In the biblical story of Jericho, spies had secretly entered Jericho before the marching began. Rahab hid those spies, and although the account was not crystal clear, she must have known those spies held a ray of hope. She knew Jericho would be destroyed, yet she begged for freedom for her and her family. Out of the kindness of their hearts, as payment for protecting their spy mission, the spies agreed to spare her and her family provided she hung a *scarlet cord* to identify her home location. Those spies might have seen Rahab as some insignificant prostitute and considered her rescue just as meaningless. But the living God had preordained it differently. He had His eye on Rahab. Rahab was physically freed from Jericho, just as the spies had promised, yet the greater aspect was Rahab's ultimate spiritual freedom. Rahab ended up in the bloodline of Jesus Christ. Just imagine her excitement when she saw and heard those massive walls tumble in a minute. The people simply shouted on the day they were instructed to do so. God caused the tumbling, and He received all the credit.

I woke up the next morning, and nothing was familiar. The outdoors appeared different. The rooms in my home seemed unfamiliar. I walked in a new land, with one certainty: I could not pack for my trip the next day.

Mary Jane called me that morning, and I did not say a word about what had occurred. She asked if we could briefly get together. As I sat across the table with my Diet Coke, she looked me square in the eye and said, "Two doors are before you, Cari, and I believe you will choose rightly." My only comment was "I believe I will." Dumbfounded and off kilter, I did not breathe a word about what had happened.

That night, Rhoda returned home, perplexed at my lack of readiness for our trip. I shook like a leaf. I knew this was the time to convey my God encounter. We sat down, and I said that I could not do this anymore and further clarified that "no more" meant no more being with women, no more gay relationships, and this was the end of us.

In her horror, she stood up and said, "So you are telling me God talked to you? You are telling me that you are putting God before our relationship?"

"Yes, I believe I am," I bravely replied.

Those words pierced through for all the powers of hell to hear, and Satan and his crew were not happy. The spewing that came forth from Rhoda's mouth in just a few short minutes caused a shuddering in me like none other. Since she knew our relationship had been on the rocks, she indicated I was using God as the excuse to break up. I made it clear that was far from the truth, but no argument would satisfy her.

Frightened, I rose, grabbed my coat and keys, and drove to the church. I wore flip-flops despite the snow. I did not care. I knew that Mary Jane and my good friend Brigette were in choir rehearsal. Looking horribly disheveled, I entered the lobby and asked a young man where the singers were practicing. He could clearly see by my face that I had been crying, and the flip-flops indicated I had been in a hurry. He guided me through the curtains at the back of the sanctuary to the doors of the choir room.

The minute I walked through those curtains, Brigette and Mary Jane walked out the choir doors. Only God could orchestrate that they were the first ones out the door, *together*. I dropped to the floor, sobbing, and shared with them the tremendous work the Lord Jesus had accomplished the night before. I kept saying, "I don't know how to live this new life."

What a time that was for all three of us. Not only had God healed me, but He had answered their deep prayers, those prayers of my dear mom, and those of the unknown warriors in the crowd.

Rhoda moved to the downstairs bedroom, and Mary Jane invited me to her family gathering for Thanksgiving. Though elation and hardship marked the next few months, I shared my newfound freedom with anyone who would hear it. My job required travel, and no matter who sat next to me, I made sure they asked just the right question when I indicated I was a transplant from Los Angeles to Ohio: "How do you like Ohio?" This was the perfect setup for me to respond, "Ohio changed my life." Then I proceeded to share the miracle the Lord had done.

On one occasion, the plane was delayed, which annoyed me. I sat in the exit row, and the seat next to me was empty. The flight attendant, fatigued from standing, sat down next to me. Our conversation started casual, but I was bursting at the seams. Then the opportunity arrived. That plane was supposed to be delayed only forty-five minutes. Instead it stayed on the tarmac for two hours, and we talked the whole time. My animation and joy spilled out all over her. Toward the end, she told me her family was struggling and she had asked God to show her a miracle so she would be able to believe. That day, my life change was her little miracle. She cried and hugged me, and we were both grateful that God had broken the plane. (I have not changed my attitude with travel or airport lounges. People still hear my story to this day.)

Swearing had always intrigued me. My language had been horrific, and I'd frequently tried to stop and even apologized when I slipped up in the wrong company. I'd not been overt about it at church though—I did have some scruples. However, swearing issued from the darkness in my heart. Without my noticing, a curious thing happened after November 23, 2009. My language changed, and I no longer swore habitually.

The task to nudge Rhoda to move forward was not an easy one. Brigette and Rhoda's mentor stayed close, still burdened that Rhoda would also have a deep encounter with the Lord. I worked diligently to find her a place to live, and she secured a little home nearby. But her move created a dilemma. My home had no ceiling lights. Rhoda had a condition called *sundowners*, in which a person reacts to fading light. We had stationed lamps everywhere, and when the sun started to set each night, all the lights in the house had to be turned on. None of the lamps were mine. I had given her quite a bit of money and had few funds left to fill in home-interior gaps left by her departure.

Someone suggested a thrift store in Tallmadge might have what I needed. I drove my Honda Accord in the snow, walked in, and asked the little old lady if they had lamps. She said I was in luck because two people had just emptied their home of all their lamps. Since it was the Christmas season, she had marked them down 50 percent. I smiled and looked to the heavens and said, "Jesus, you are just too good." I loaded my car with twelve beautiful lamps and shades, and I drove home praising the Lord for His provision. I strategically placed them in the house, turned them on, and screamed, "Let there be light."

I considered myself unskilled at decorating, and Rhoda had gladly underscored my lack on multiple occasions. My tabletops, countertops, kitchen, and curio cabinets went from cluttered to empty. Yet God gave me the eyes to buy art, dishes, and tchotchkes to reset the home to my taste. It was all Him, and He did a nice job. I had space to breathe, and cleaning was far easier.

Rhoda eventually left the area, and I was not certain where she stood with the Lord. I could only pray, as did others, knowing God is never finished with us until we are dead.

I now knew the love of God and the power of God. God had defeated the untamable beast. God removed the thread that had woven itself in every part of my framework and bound up my soul. It could not touch my spirit (the space reserved for God and God alone). Praise Him for that. The freedom I received was to live for Christ fully, outside the wall that He tumbled to the ground. He afforded a clear path to the good land of His ultimate purpose for my life. He also wanted 100 percent.

On Super Bowl Sunday 2010, the Lord woke me up well in advance of my normal time to prepare for church. While I soaked in my tub, He graciously reminded me I still had a holdout. I had not shared my testimony with Leslie. I knew in my heart I had to email her before church, and I had time. I poured out with rigorous honesty all the Lord had done in my life and officially closed the door on any future romantic prospect. My physical obedience to the Lord was set. But God saw the deeper tie in my heart that had to be cut in full surrender to Him. My tear-filled eyes embraced my Savior as I let go of the psychological tie that could no longer have a place in my life. About two weeks later, I received a wonderful response. That same day she met someone, as I had "freed her" to move on with her own journey. Although a difficult read, I worshiped the Lord for all He had done, and He met me in the most loving way.

Although Leslie and I had never met, we maintained our friendship, not in a romantic love but one of honesty and intimacy with boundaries. I knew she was in my life for reasons beyond human understanding. I prayed for her and her family, as she had struggled through a series of harsh tragedies with her precious daughter. I appreciated the relational honesty and the depth of friendship from afar that God allowed, even though I initially pursued it from a broken place. God never said we could not have intimate and deep friendships, and He continued to bless me with many more.

Baptism

Given my new freedom in Christ, I felt compelled to be baptized in March 2009. Although I had been in the waters once before in the LC, this wholeness in Christ and the reality of who I was in Him gripped me. He engraved my name on the cross, He took my struggle to the grave, and most importantly, He defeated it through the resurrection. This would be my declaration to the whole world and to the powers of hell that I belonged to the Lord. The old gay Cari would remain in those waters, and the new Cari, whom God had seen before time, was beginning a brand-new chapter. I had a heightened sensitivity to life and to people, and best of all, there were no more missing puzzle pieces. He'd made me whole.

That day in the water was a glorious moment as the congregation sang "Mighty to Save." I leaped and smiled in those waters, as the Lord had granted me the deepest desire of my heart. My dear mother and my best friend in California witnessed it on live-stream video. I imagined the joy in my mother's heart. She had prayed for decades and even years prior to my actual declaration of "I am a lesbian." Now there I stood, consecrated to the Lord and free from the untamable beast in my soul. What a testament to answered prayer and praying until the prayer is answered.

My baptism grew legs. Almost overnight I went from unknown to known. That presented a challenge, as I knew the face of pride, and it scared me. I had lived in the city of Hudson and hardly knew anyone. Now, no matter where I went—the coffee shop, the grocery store, a restaurant—people stopped me on the street and said, "I saw your baptism!" The video of it traveled all over the country. Few people vocally declare coming out of homosexuality, especially in northeast Ohio, and people expressed excitement about a changed life. I was grateful that so many were encouraged by the Lord. Homosexuality has hit just about every family structure on some level. Therefore, I embraced the fact that God's glory was declared that day and His work in a life must be shared with others.

However, the Enemy was mad, and he never rests, and the sin that caused him to fall was pride. I knew that pride banged on my door in the weeks to follow. I felt like a mini-celebrity. I had been healed of homosexuality, but I still struggled with an identity issue, and I had massive amounts of growing left to do. Satan positioned his next move. He is not bigger than God but is as deceptive as a crouching lion, ready to stomp out anything the Lord has accomplished.

Sitting by my bed one night, I asked God to simmer the publicity. I could not handle it. It fed my pride, and I knew it deep in my soul. I knew the Word. I declared audibly in Jesus's name for all the powers of hell to be shut. The healing I received was God's doing. But in the mix, some of the praises had an element of serious redirect away from God. The Lord answered my prayer, and the exposure slowed.

Pride always knocks at the door. A minister once told a story in which, following his message, a man told him what a fabulous job he had done. The minister replied, "Yes, the Enemy has already told me that." I realize, even in the writing of this book, that this is God's call, and the laying down of my flesh will be constant until I meet Him in glory. However, I also embrace the woman at the well who ran into that city and told everything the Lord had done. That is exactly what I have been called to do as well, and it is incredibly exciting!

And the woman from Panera Bread? As God would ordain, she and I met each other shortly after my baptism. What a testimony this was to her. She'd been convinced she had failed miserably in the encounter with me. But God always gets His way. We humans may not do everything perfectly. We are to simply be obedient, and God will do the rest. It was such a blessing for me to be able to thank this woman for being faithful.

The day I was baptized, I wrote this poem. It depicts my healing and the few months that followed baptism day.

Miraculous

How does one bottle a moment in time?
When into God's arms, I humbly resign.
Love transferred down, I am healed at the core
My hands open wide, "Oh Lord, what's in store?"
I traveled the corners of unruly hate
Yet in my anguish, the Son could relate.
Inside His deep eyes my history was told

Jericho Unmasked

Unmatched protection so my soul was not sold.
I chased with such longing, the beauty of love
Yet constantly brushed by wings of the Dove.
Wiping my eyes to clear out the blur
Turning up noises to drown out the stir
With swiftness of feet, I ran my own way
In the night's stillness, I'd begged you to stay.
A thread of the false propelled through my veins
Yet you untied knots, and your stitches remained.
Was my name on the cross, or was I forgotten?
Was my struggle excluded from His walk, the Begotten?
So precise and detailed with hands that don't harm
Yet a voice that went quiet, the sound of alarm.
Hallways of idols, all crumbling in rubble
I groped through the pieces as you foretold trouble.
Kneeling in ruins amid all the dross
A thin page from your Word, a vision, the cost.
We wept in such concert as you breathed forth my name
The impact a shock and I wouldn't be the same.
You tilled my soul's soil with new seeds to reap
And watered with grace as I went to sleep.
You gathered the friends and linked them in prayer
A unified army, strong borders of care.
You lit up old habits that could not belong
Peace was restored when I claimed they were wrong.
I'm one among many in the sea of the broken
May this God carve more futures through what will be spoken.

My Dear Elizabeth

In 2009 Elizabeth was eighteen and had graduated from a Catholic high school. Two weeks after the Lord healed me and I was walking in consecration to Him, I received a call from her. She informed me that she had started the Alcoholics Anonymous program. She knew where her life was headed and wanted to make a dramatic change. I took a huge breath and knew the Lord was up to something. I did not dare make a big deal of it, but inside I praised Jesus that He had His hand on her and always would. She'd been dedicated to Him as a baby, and He had His eye on her. Deuteronomy 30:19 came alive in my heart that day: "I call heaven and earth to witness against you today, that I have set before you life and death, the blessing and the curse. So choose life in order that you may live, you and your descendants."

My parenting skills had fallen drastically short of all that God intended. I had put so many other people in first place to fill the hole inside, and unfortunately, Elizabeth suffered. The partners I'd selected magnified the chaos. A year after the Lord freed me, Elizabeth called and named all I had done wrong, including my move to Ohio her senior year of high school. I knew from the depths of my heart not to defend. With tears, I told her she was right about everything except one. God had lifted me out of Los Angeles and brought me to Ohio. This had not been a parenting issue—it had been God ordained.

At the end of our dialogue, I shared the importance of forgiveness. She knew what had happened between her dad and me, so I conveyed that the Lord had forgiven me of my deplorable mistakes and lack in fully treasuring the gift He had blessed me with on January 27, 1991. I shared my prayer for her, which encompassed the hope that she would find the same forgiveness I had given to her dad, and ultimately, that she would forgive me. I figured she hadn't expected me to speedily admit failure and take responsibility. I didn't include a single "but" statement in my sentences. I did not blame circumstances, my divorce, or any other event that might have provided an excuse. However, I believed unforgiveness would consume her, and my desire was that she be set free.

Several months later I received another call. God had graced her with the gift of forgiveness, and a brand-new mother-daughter journey launched.

Elizabeth and I have a special connection and unique dynamic. She is the dear daughter who was a built-in source of grounding and protection when I lived in rebellion. If I had not had a child, life would have been far worse. The Enemy would have capitalized on entirely too much freedom. There were wonderful and precious times with her. Peter and Jim both stood by me through many of the traumas of lost relationships. We have a deep friendship to this day. I have shared my testimony with each of them, and I know Elizabeth sees the change. I want to be the praying mom that my mother exemplified and still does at ninety-two years old.

Elizabeth is now a twenty-seven-year-old with amazing wisdom and character. She is on her own journey, and I honor what God has done and will do in her life in His time. She received the Lord at a young age. I saw her face and her eyes when He entered her spirit. I know He sees the end from the beginning and that His promises are true, yet I hold her with an open hand and pray daily that her walk will encompass deep intimacy with the Lord. I still drive her nuts in a good way, but now I am there for her in wholeness. God is first, and she knows that. I try not to preach. Instead I attempt to guide, listen, and lead when asked. We keep short accounts, and I am glad she has her voice to speak as a young woman. I love her deeply and am in awe of how the Lord fearfully and wonderfully made her. I am utterly blessed that the Lord Jesus chose me as her mother.

Chapter 15

A Deeper Commitment

God's work on November 23, 2009, was nothing short of miraculous. However, the next step had an even deeper impact. A number of months later, my pastor handed me a document about walking in freedom and wholeness in Christ in the midst of a homosexual struggle. A particularly compelling portion referenced Christ's worth even if it meant laying down any prospects of sexual intimacy. It underscored the premise that a person who embraced this call would experience faces of God that no one else would see and would one day meet the Lord in eternity and realize it was all worth it.

It was Sunday morning when I landed on those pages, and the Lord spoke. *Cari, may I have all of you?* I dropped to the floor facedown and sobbed. Since my love language was touch, I had a hard time being alone. This request was huge. God knew I had been dabbling online looking at dating sites, thinking I might find a Christian man. I even went on a few dates but was stressed most of the time. I was trying to fit in, as I lived in a community of almost all couples, so there was tremendous emphasis in the church life on marriage. I was still in the infancy stage toward the deeper work of identity, so God intervened fast and furiously. He knew what was best for me, and dating was not His best.

That day I surrendered my entire future to the Lord, even if it meant that no man would be in my future on a romantic level. How did this obedience translate? It was a complete laying down of my love language and entrusting it to His care. It was a declaration that He was enough and worth the cost. God's direction was holiness, and I had started to convolute that path with something not in His transformation equation. Yet now it was God's mission, not mine. Praise Him.

I am still walking single before Him nine years later, and I would not have it any other way. I treasure the way I can solely focus on Him without distraction. I honor marriage, but I also view my singleness as a gift from the Father.

After that encounter, I had scanned cards in the Hallmark store the following February and felt a longing and sadness in my heart and thought, *I have no valentine.* The next day I spent time with the Lord in His Word, and this poem graced my heart. He was enough, even in the solitude, and this was a huge miracle.

VALENTINE

"My Valentine!" The color red, the cards aligned to hail
Yet yours the voice poetic, as all the others pale.
Conveyance on a spectrum, mere friend to deep romance
Yet penmanship of sacrifice rests deep within your glance.
Their gift one heartfelt moment, the table linens placed
Yet pain, regret, and hardship their message can't erase.
Your letter is delivered with hands unlike another
And as I turn the pages, it's you I soon discover.
Not simply just a verse soon hidden out of sight
Oh, yours I must reread as they mark out such might.
And as I canvas pages, the words weave in my slumber
Your breath my very comfort, your touch is what I hunger.
What Valentine is this who knows my every part
Yet so compelled to seek me on paths I tried to chart.
You saw me with no other, all lovers cut like knives
Yet blanketed with mercy, rich crystals are your eyes.
As I awoke this morning so hugged by arms of grace

You cupped my cheeks so tightly. "Oh, Cari, don't replace.

My love design and pierced-through hands afford me all the right

Just open yours and don't pull back, as my grip will be tight.

I'll call you into places where you'll be very scared

But none void of my presence, the masses never dared.

My desire, your commitment and courage quite unmatched

And as you press in deeper, my heart to you unlatched.

I'm coming soon to claim my bride and take her to my chamber

Yet down that aisle as she draws near, it won't be void of danger.

Today you have my letter—keep reading. It's my heart

And press in to my glory, your obedience each day's start!"

Network of Accountability and Friendship

John 11:43–44 says, "And when He had said these things, He cried out with a loud voice, 'Lazarus, come forth.' He who had died came forth, bound hand and foot with wrappings; and his face was wrapped around with a cloth. Jesus said to them, 'Unbind him, and let him go.'"

Jesus said to the *people*, "Unbind him and let him go." The Lord freed me and healed me, yet I was still bound in "grave clothes." I needed others to spiritually and relationally help unwrap all that had bound me for so long, especially the wrong, deep-embedded concepts of Christ that I'd adopted in the LC. The barrage of concepts regarding reward and punishment had plagued my past and propelled many outward attempts to change my behavior. I needed to be unwrapped of these fallen impressions of God and false images of intimacy. I needed to be unwrapped to walk free in Christ. Yes, of course Christ is all in all. But He also called us to walk this journey with the body of Christ, to hold one another up, to apply the healing balm of grace when we falter, to challenge one another in love, and to put on display for all the world to see our oneness in Him.

The Lord placed me smack dab in the middle of a church home group with four married couples who had been soaking in the Word for years. Little did I know before I landed in this group that they had prayed for Rhoda and me from the time we arrived at the church. This was such a blessing. They saw what the Lord Jesus saw, a freed woman, yet still requiring more transformation.

Although my healing was massive, I didn't hunger for His Word. I rose in the morning and gave Him fifteen minutes with a little devotional. Then I scanned the Scriptures for my "pill" for the day.

Provincetown

Although I had been taken out of darkness into the light, I stayed in contact with some of my gay friends, including a couple in Boston, Jane and Bianca. Jane had suffered breast cancer and was on the mend, and she begged me to visit her cabin. I thought nothing of it, excited to see her again. This caused a panic in my home group, as they understood the danger of walking into this situation. They prayed in silence, and off I went. I truly appreciated this response, as I was good with rules and adapting to others—however, it was imperative that my walk with God be from the inside out.

I traveled innocently to Massachusetts to a beach town about forty-five minutes from Provincetown.

I arrived at the cabin, and after they showed me around, I unpacked in my assigned bedroom upstairs. Jane had said that the next day we would partner in bartending a big lesbian party for a friend. Immediately I heard the Lord's voice so strong with 2 Corinthians 6:17: "Therefore, come out from their midst and be separate, says the Lord." It stunned me, but it cut me right to the core, and I knew this weekend would not be what I had anticipated. I was distressed at that party.

Ironically, prior to Jane's breast cancer, she had visited my home in California and had been in a desperate state. I had shared the gospel message with her one morning, and she'd received Christ.

It was powerful at the time. Though I'd been walking in darkness then, God worked in a mysterious way and in an unlikely setting.

The day following the bartending experience, Jane and I sat on the porch, reminiscing about life. As I was a guest in their home, I shared cautiously, not out of fear but from a sensitive place, as my testimony would have flown in the face of their entire life as a couple. There was no denying that I did not look the same as I had during my last visit with her. My face was different. My countenance was different. I had been altered on the inside, and my outward appearance reflected the change.

Jane kept pressing me. "You are not the same. What is going on?"

It got so over the top that I balanced on the precipice of denying the Lord if I kept quiet. With trembling in my heart, I conveyed the details of my healing experience. I underscored that it was my testimony and not a criticism or judgment of her. I was gentle, yet excited, as sharing caused a pumping through my veins and invoked a smile from ear to ear.

Her face did not mirror my smile. "You are like a bad odor," she said.

To defuse the situation, I simply laughed and said, "Well, I did shower this morning." We made it through to the other side, agreeing to disagree, but it was a treacherous and scary journey, one exemplified by 2 Corinthians 2:15–16: "For we are a fragrance of Christ to God among those who are being saved and among those who are perishing; to the one an aroma from death to death, to the other an aroma from life to life."

Jane and Bianca had planned a short road trip to Provincetown, Massachusetts, one of the gay meccas of the United States. Given that the Lord insisted I "come out and be separate," I was pressed that this road trip was not in His plan. Luke 17:32—"Remember Lot's wife"—drummed in my ear. When the Lord burned up Sodom and Gomorrah as a result of sin and treachery, He had mercy on Lot and his family. The Lord pulled them out and spared them.

They were called to run away from the burning town with their eyes fixed on what was ahead. However, Lot's wife looked back on the city, defying the command, and turned into a pillar of salt. My "looking" at Provincetown would be a "looking back" of sorts.

The night before we were supposed to go, I prayed in the privacy of the room for the Lord to move heaven and earth on my behalf. I did not want to be disobedient to Him, but I did not have the courage to decline an invitation to an event that Jane and Bianca had been planning for weeks. The Lord gave me deep peace that night.

The next morning, while I was preparing coffee, Bianca came into the kitchen and said that Jane had had a bad night and the plans would have to be canceled. I felt horrible that Jane was sick, but I struggled to hide the joy in my spirit that God had answered my prayers. The day before, Jane and I had gone kayaking, so it wasn't as if she had already been in a weakened state when I arrived. I went back upstairs, looked in the mirror with tears flowing down, and said, "Thank you, Jesus, for taking care of me." What love the Father displayed that day! I also knew Provincetown was a city I would never see.

This did not end the dilemmas though.

Jane and Bianca were planning a wedding, and I was on the guest list. Bianca's father was a pastor in a Baptist church, so Bianca picked up on some things with me that Jane did not see or chose to overlook because of our relationship. Jane shared my story with her, and it unleashed Bianca's anger, as she had an extreme hatred of Christianity. The last day of my visit was innocuous, but I could not wait to get home. At this juncture in my walk with the Lord, this was not where I was supposed to be, and the Lord would not let me be cozy. They drove me to the bus, and I prayed the entire ninety-minute ride to the Boston airport, asking the Lord to move on my behalf so I would not have to return to their wedding. I believed with my whole heart that the Lord would work it out. I just did not know how fast it would be.

While waiting for my flight, I received a call from Jane. Her tone had changed dramatically, and she delivered a verbal lashing challenging me on every level, including an assessment that I was deceived and delusional. Closing remarks included the declaration that they wanted no part of my life and it was the end. Although shaking and sad for the loss of friendship with Jane, I knew that God had answered my prayer again. He held my heart through those moments of tears and embraced me tight as I flew home.

I later found out that my home group had been praying for me and for my protection. Thank heavens for such deep care.

God's Expansion of the Net

I had country club friends and the home group, yet God expanded the net of relationships, which mainly contained female friends. Developing friendships was difficult at first, as I'd had only a couple of straight friends in Los Angeles when I departed, so the majority of past relationships with women were framed in a fallen concept of intimacy.

One struggle when coming out of the gay lifestyle was the risk that female friends would perceive that there was an attraction. One could be vulnerable to false assessments or misunderstandings. I saw this as ego run rampant. Lesbians were not attracted to everyone in a "skirt," and unlike many in the lesbian community, I never mixed friends and lovers, as that was weird, in my mind. But it appeared to be the norm in many lesbian circles. Needless to say, the words "I love you" did not just roll off my tongue, and I proceeded with caution when it came to physical touch. (I am sometimes still shy about physical touch.)

God blessed me with a small circle of intimate friends. They mentored me, pointed me to Christ, invited me to dinners and hikes, and extended their lives to include me. This was a massive gift, as God answered the place of loneliness in me and established a strong network of accountability. I not only had a responsibility to the Lord, but it extended to the body of Christ.

Worship was a central theme with those in my close circle. They welcomed me in their gatherings of singing, rejoicing, and praising the Lord. I experienced moments that took my breath away, and that worship recarved my view of the Lord.

One New Year's Eve 2011, I joined five other ladies at an all-night worship from 6:00 p.m. to 6:00 a.m., a vertical worship to the Father with no discussion among each other, just intimacy with God. When we arrived, we set up our resting mats along the walls of the large auditorium, and the music started. Unsure of what to do, I watched and observed. This setting offered many firsts, as it was also the first time I had put on a dress in years. After a few hours, I abandoned my shyness and started to dance with Jesus. All my senses were heightened as I praised and worshiped and focused on just Him. He restored my soul, and when I rested, I lay in green pastures. The mere thought of doing this for eternity consumed my heart, and I knew I was made for this, for worship. Jesus was leading, and later I composed this poem.

THE DANCE

There I sat so alone and lost in a crowd
Others stood confident in finery so proud.
You approached from a distance, I so unaware
The lights were all flashing as I hid from the glare.
So young and so clumsy my feet unprepared
You said, "Just relinquish. Try not to be scared."
My movements unskilled as I tried to lead
But as I exhausted, I'd finally concede.
Then exit and rest while the music still played
As notes formed an encore, but I was afraid.
I quickly grabbed baggage and ran clinging tight
And dismissed the whole setting as casual and trite.
There on the pillow tracing lines of His smile

The touch and the voice, my mind's memory did file.
During weeks, months, and years, I'd rehearse all alone
And choreograph movements I claimed as my own.
He approached once again, and I rose with such ease
So suddenly paralyzed, my heart He did seize.
Was this the same one that the lights had so blinded?
Yet eyes told the story as I was reminded.
In anticipation, I'd predict the next step
But He'd whisper so softly, first release the regret.
One foot would move forward while the other held back
Compelled by control, claiming history as fact.
Knocked back to familiar that I had rehearsed
Once again so alone as the crowds soon dispersed.
This dance floor of patterns that were seemingly random
Yet marked by His leading and a dance so in tandem.
Tread marks of those where the tiles had blackened
This dance had erased and removed their distraction.
I fell to the floor as I said, "Dance no more!"
Yet off in the distance, a voice did implore.
See this new venue, not one thing the same
But I am still here and choose to remain.
Are your hands and your feet still glued in one place?
Allow me to lift you and let my feet retrace.
Are your arms going to force in specific direction?
Or will I lead the dance with such intimate perfection?

I had been healed from homosexuality, but my thinking remained liberal, especially in the matter of pro-choice. My close friends advocated for life and knew the suffering and spiritual depravity that occurred as a result of a decision to end life. I made no bones about my stance but agreed to disagree. In kindness, they gave me a little book that was a walk through the Bible on the subject. When I landed on Revelation 12, the Lord seized my heart and I saw the dragon (Satan) standing over the woman, attempting to devour her child. As I read further, I realized that although the dragon had been unsuccessful in this particular attempt, he never stopped his mission to devour and destroy as many unique reflections of God as possible. What a frightening thought. That day my liberal thinking was dramatically altered by God's Word, not by people's feeble attempt to redirect my thinking.

The living and operative Word of God transformed my mentality. A few days later I was driving with a friend who made the small statement that "we have lost so much with the slaughtered unborn." That statement stirred in my spirit for days, and the Lord birthed a poem. Normally, my poems were written in just a few hours, but this one took days. I could not stop pondering. It was a deep work the Lord was doing to transform a mind that had been shaped by the liberal worldview.

ABORTION'S COST

God formed unending value realized long before their time
Yet all their lives were stolen, the prophetic and a sign.
Faces so unknown, now marked with such distinction
Their contribution ended by hands of mass extinction.
God reads them small short stories and novels from His heart
Yet we are robbed of endings as these lives never start.
Would disciple thirteen testify and wash our Savior's feet?
Yet hands had never birthed as heart took one last beat.
Would a voice of truth cry out against hypocritical noise?
Yet only silent whispers as masks and needles poise.
Would we face the ruin as cells merge into cancer?
Or did the laws of choice impale the very answer?
Would friend be there as suicide plagued the hopeless soul?

A Deeper Commitment

Or was compassion compromised by death an early goal?
Would slavery have prevailed, if courage did outnumber?
Or were those marked to stand attacked and forced to slumber?
Would music scores explode, inspiring spiritual dance?
If parchments had not sealed, composer had no chance.
Would homeless comb the sidewalks in filth as their disguise
If architects of missions had not met such quick demise?
Would prayers rise up like trumpets, appealing one great cause?
Or were they trapped in anguish, bound up by bloodied gauze?
Would teachers flood the ghettos, freeing young minds of their plight?
Or were they suctioned out and drowned, too small to even fight?
Would color splash the walls of churches large and small?
Yet black seeps in the cracks, there's less who hear the call.
Would politicians rise unchecked, bring glory to themselves?
Yet wisdom marked those key ones, their cradles harshly shelved.
Would borders have to soften as population crowded?
"Premature" the concept as young are tossed or shrouded.
Would the woman be abused by one she thought so fine?
Yet he who would have honored never got the chance to dine.
Would men regret the anguish, their wives resigned with grief?
And walk the streets of loneliness with prostitutes repeat?
Would psychology be reckoned with a biblical advantage
Yet those who would have mined for truth, bled out with scars unbandaged?
Would Gospel spread to regions where most have never dared?
Or were the mighty soldiers disarmed as infants scared?
We could continue scripting, ponder all we'd rearrange
Or set our sight on life, seize options launching change.
One day we'll meet them all, perfection we'll behold
The glisten of their smiles will mute the streets of gold.

My life was so full. What could be better? My bravery increased with saying "I love you," and sometimes I probably said it too much. But I meant it from my heart. God had wired me to be relational, and based on my experience in the LC, I had a heightened sensitivity to people, even in the workplace. My friends were everything. I felt cared for and safe and assured I had "arrived." This next poem was not written at this juncture. But like many of my poems, they were not meant for the time they were written. They were meant for me to go back and reread at the appointed time. I thought healing from homosexuality was the end. I thought all was perfect because I had dear friends.

The Book

The journey of life so hard to explain
The losses we've felt but also great gain.
As we look back and say, "Why couldn't I have known?"
Another voice says, "But my, how you've grown."
We are born with our eyes filled with wonders and dreams
Not realizing the world of manipulation and schemes.
Rivers of people so cynical and rushed
Passing so quickly they rarely are touched.
As we float in the center, that place where it's calm,
Our eyes open wide to our friends we are drawn
As frustrations and hurts rapidly diminish,
We think to ourselves, "What a great finish!"
Then to our surprise with our hands open wide
A beautiful box with a book lands inside.
It's not unfamiliar as it's one of our own
Written descriptions of all we've been shown.
The words on the page some forgotten, some lost
Buried behind what we thought was great cost.

A Deeper Commitment

So unexpected the words come to life
New pages we turn, but they are all white.
We ponder and anticipate at what rests ahead
Still haunted by thoughts of the lies that were said.
A new image appears from the sheen on the page
Is our heart still deceived, or is this a new stage?
Amid all the risk and with silent reserve
The pen's in His hand—let the journey emerge.

Chapter 16

Identity

I sat in a Bible study on the book of Jonah, and someone spoke a sentence that stuck with me: "The greatest hindrance to the next great work of God in your life is the *last* great work." No one could argue that being healed from homosexuality was nothing short of tremendous. I was free, with no opaque canvas or wall between me and the Lord. Those walls had tumbled down, and I walked in the Sonlight. Still, insecurities riddled my life, and I did not set good boundaries. My identity was still wrapped in what people thought of me, and my capacity to blend in a group was unmatched. I no longer lived in a fallen state of homosexuality, but I was emotionally attached to my friends. Instead of deeply pursuing the Word on my own, I could glean from "thus saith my friends." After all, these strong Christians knew best. My friends were, and still are, 911s of strength. But God is a jealous God, and He will have no idols before Him. I was about to enter one of the greatest turning points in my life, the journey toward *identity in Him.*

God sovereignly arranged to remove some of my friends from my life for a season. This did not please me one bit. I cried and screamed to the Lord because I was so angry. I initially bought the lie from the Enemy that my intimacy and heart had been misperceived as homosexual and that was why they went away. The Lord in His grace, though, did not remove everyone. Some walked closely alongside, encouraging me and pointing me to Christ. Words could not describe how the separation from the others tore at my soul. Unknowingly, I had made something bigger than Christ, but I was unable to see it. Blinded by such a miraculous healing, I failed to recognize that the Lord wanted to transform every part and bring me to wholeness in Him where He had first place in my heart.

My fight went on for months. I begged and pleaded for reconciliation, to no avail. I dove into the Word of God like never before, no longer spending just the fifteen "hi and bye" minutes in the morning. Now, I rose early and spent time out of desperation. I pored over the Word with deep tears of loss that I could not understand on any level. It hit the core of rejection and abandonment that I had experienced too many times, and the broken triggers in my heart fired on all cylinders. I felt like the Lord had cut me down to nothing. This was a pruning away like none other.

The Enemy stayed too close by, always whispering false accusations in my ear.

The Lord, however, gifted me with an amazing Christian therapist. I did not know why I entered those rooms at first, because therapy had never helped in the past. It had only made things worse. I made it clear at the onset that I was not interested in archeological digs, parent bashing, or any other traditional therapeutic technique. I was surprised she agreed to provide counsel, considering my daunting list of don'ts. I also made sure not a bone in her body would condone my prior homosexual life, or worse yet, suggest I should accept homosexuality as the reality of who I am. One might think it obvious that this would be the position of a Christian therapist. I felt it critical to check though. I had witnessed compromise bleeding into Christian circles at a rapid pace, and this idea of "born gay, so embrace it" was hitting parents hard, especially with those who had sons and daughters who'd declared themselves gay. This is where the Enemy hits the hardest, and it is a dangerous place for any church, or persons in the pulpit, to deviate from the Word of God and try to rename sin.

Within this safe environment, God allowed flashbacks of Uncle Max's sexual abuse to surface. He brought the memories to my consciousness in *His* way, with extreme kindness. Timidly and shamefully, I addressed it in therapy and passed through to the other side, released from the subconscious wreckage.

I'm still astounded how my mind as a child was wired to survive and dissociate from all that occurred with Uncle Max. It was as if I'd tucked it into a sealed coffin on the premise that it would eventually rot to dust. Unfortunately, my subconscious stayed very much alive. Through the prior years of therapy during my struggle with sexuality, I'd been insistent that no sexual abuse or impropriety had occurred. I could not stomach the psychology trend that everyone suffered abuse, even if they did not remember it. I felt that was implicitly tied to the power of suggestion and would get mad when the psychologist broached the subject. I did have female partners, though, who had been victims. I'd also encountered a couple of teens who shared their stories, after which, when on a plane and contemplating the entire topic, I was compelled to write. I grabbed napkins and a pen, and the following poem sprung out, written in the summer of 2005, years prior to the horrific realization within the safety of a godly therapist and Jesus.

HOPE

Hidden inside with so little to say
Pierced in the soul by a thin jagged ray.
Innocence of youth marred by rejection
Yet all you seek is untainted affection.
Haunted by flashbacks of visitors at night
Armies of terror as in silence you fight.
Eyes closed but open as you travel the distance
Yet you are paralyzed by lack of resistance.
Hands reaching out to the ones you should trust
Those filled with demons of violence and lust.
As the years pass, the dreams turn to anger
Walls have erected as mirrors of danger.

One knocks at the door, but you won't let them in
An encore performance might happen again.
Other hearts open with a love that is kind
Yet the hole in your soul has conquered your mind.
The prisoner inside is feeding the hate
While lack of control has made you irate.
Finally, one day the sun finds a crack
In total amazement you're forced to step back.
The clock's in reverse, the memories too real
Healing's begun, but you are forced to feel.
Ego and esteem so foreign at best
Yet as you proceed they're no longer just guests.
Vengeance and shame combined with self-hate
Then love and forgiveness, you start to relate.
It seemed so unfair that so much had happened
Yet you had the guts to risk and take action.
Robbed and so plundered at such a young age
Yet in adulthood they couldn't keep you caged.
Power inside that you claimed as your own
A miracle walks, the example you've shown.
None can explain the tragedies in life
Why some have it easy and some with great strife.
Yet in that moment at the brink of our doom
We make the choice to let light fill the room.
No longer hidden, the soul breaks forth a blossom
On a road of recovery, a freedom that's awesome.

At the time, I was stunned by what I had composed. My other poems had been representations of me. Why was this one different? When I shared it with others, I highlighted that it was *not* about me. Yet years later, in God's divine timing, this poem was no longer a guest of my life but implicit to my life. I said, "Thank you, Jesus, for birthing in me what you knew you would do, even before I saw it!" It is now one of my favorite compositions.

God could not have used the therapy in my life to the degree that He had if I had not been spending intimate one-on-one time with Him in His Word. He will have *no* other idol, and by God's grace I had not made therapy an idol. My therapist was (and is) a treasure in my life. The depths of my therapy remained in the confines of the safe space, yet the outcome had been steady and radical transformation. I was blessed beyond measure and learned proper boundaries, what was mine to own and what deserved to be discarded as false. Most of all, the definition of God's love and human intimacy was redefined properly. Therapy positively impacted my choices, bolstered the Word of God and His sovereignty, and reinforced freedom and courage to proceed on this journey at the Lord's pace, not man's pace.

I developed a habit that I treasure. No matter what time I have to wake up in the morning, I make sure the Lord gets first place with quality time. Corporate and individual prayers, tears, and transformation have occurred in my two sanctuaries: the couch in my office where I first received healing and my gazebo in the summer, listening to a gentle flowing waterfall.

Another key moment was when a dear friend invited me to view a short film in her home called *The Potter: Reflections of a Master Artisan* (Day of Discovery production). She knew my identity struggle intimately and wanted me to see a powerful example of God's detailed plan for my life. The film was a demonstration by a Christian potter. He formed the clay on his own potter's wheel while showing step by step the process of making a clay pot. In the beginning, the potter formed the pot. It actually looked good and shapely. The potter's hand *never* left the clay. If his hands had released, the clay would have become wobbly and imbalanced and splattered off the wheel. Shortly into the demonstration, he pounded the formed clay pot down to a flattened state. I could not believe my eyes. The pot had looked good. Why was he pounding it down to its seemingly original form? He said the pounding was required to remove any air bubbles. If he had not done this pounding and reshaping, those air bubbles would have caused the pot to explode as soon as it was placed in the fiery kiln. That potter relentlessly pounded. When he started the reforming process, he drove his entire fist and arm down into the center and pulled out all the dross.

When I saw this, I cried. I realized I needed to be lovingly pounded down by the Lord. In His mercy He could not create just a nice pot loaded with air gaps only to subsequently explode when trials hit. I would not be equipped to withstand the tide of this age and would crumble under the pressure. There would be no stamina to walk with the Lord in the manner He called me to walk. This freed me to recognize that I was exactly where I was supposed to be in His divine plan. This short film taught me that the finished pot was always in the potter's eye, just like I had been the apple of God's eye.

Finding true identity in Christ will be a lifetime of transformation. Daily, many things tug at my heart, not to mention that I am my own little idol factory. However, communion with Him every morning and constant engagement throughout the day, even in the smallest of endeavors, keep His smile and eyes at the forefront. Trust increases, the relationship with Him continues to grow stronger, and the desire for His best continues to become the major, instead of the minor, quest.

Restoration of Vertical Order

The gay games were coming to Cleveland in the summer of 2014. Several months before the event, I met with a group of men and women who had been praying since October 2008. The divine hand of God came to focus as I chronologically scrolled back to the time some of the women had started to pray.

In October of 2008, the Federation of Gay Games announced that Cleveland was one of four cities being considered for the games.

This was the exact month and year that I arrived in Ohio. Women had started to fervently pray that Cleveland would not be selected. Many churches also rose up to pray. Some of the families had gay children or gay relatives and had become discouraged. People were coming out of the closet, but news was not spreading of gay people being healed and called to serve the Lord. September 29, 2009, was when I'd heard the pastor's message on Galatians, and this was also the month the news announced Cleveland had been selected to host the gay games. What an amazing God we serve that He designed the message that last weekend of September!

I believe those prayers in October 2008 were instrumental in the initial shake-up of my life. From the time I got a job offer to the time I unpacked in Ohio, less than twenty days had passed. Subsequently, God knew I would be healed and would eventually be the encouragement that these women needed. Prior to the start of the games in 2014, I wrote an email to one of the ladies, who is now a dear friend:

God has answered your prayers. You may think that He did not because Cleveland was selected, yet behind the scenes, I am the outcome of the prayers. God is raising up those to fight on behalf of those enslaved. He got the bride in Cleveland to pray. The Father is developing a strong army and drawing those, even moving those to Cleveland, that you cannot see. But they will be on the front lines sharing the gospel message because the Lord has healed them and called them, and your prayers have been instrumental. I thank Him that every Friday night you all prayed and continue to pray. Be encouraged. He is a personal God. Why are the games coming here? Because behind all the show there are cries of deep tears. God has challenged us to have eyes to see the brokenness. He came to bind up the brokenhearted and set the captives free. We pray against the Enemy that would attempt to destroy life to the uttermost. But God is bringing an unlikely harvest, and I wanted to tell you firsthand—don't stop praying. There are more "me's" out there. My new friend, be blessed, encouraged, and honored that the Father has used you and will use you further as you pray, watch, and expect the utter amazing to happen—*it will.*

Throughout the months leading up to the games, I was introduced to several people who had also been healed. Oh, the joy in my heart to meet men and woman with similar experiences. I connected with other solid believers and developed many more friendships. My prayer life went into high gear as we walked the streets of Cleveland for hours, praying for the ground and everyone who would step off the plane. A deep love evolved through the prayers. As some of us conveyed our own stories, it added a much-needed personal component, as we were real people with real lives and real struggles, but still created to bring God glory. His heart longed for the many. Second Peter 3:9 states, "The Lord is not slow about his promise as some count slowness, but is patient toward you, not wishing for any to perish, but for all to come to repentance."

One evening, while praying for the gay games, a missionary from Africa spoke regarding the headship of Christ in relation to the church. During that message, God opened my eyes to the divine vertical order that He set forth in Genesis. It was God, then man, then woman. I knew this did not mean that woman was inferior to man. Rather, God had set a covering in place. In the garden, Eve walked away from the covering of Adam and listened to Satan's subtle questions. Adam was not any better, because he looked on and failed to cover Eve. Then both Adam and Eve came out from under the headship and covering of God. What a picture this was for me, as I had concluded years earlier that I did not need a man in my life. I was just fine on my own. That mantra did not stop after I was healed. There might be moments when I thought it would be nice to have a guy around for heavy lifting. However, I was industrious, so even that was not a hindrance. As I listened to the missionary, I realized how fallen that attitude was in my own heart because it dismissed the divine order. My perspective changed. I acquired an increased appreciation for the men in my home group and all the men in the church. I was called to honor them in a deep and rich way. In my heart that night, the living God restored a vertical order. Recognition of this was also key to my identity growth. God, in His infinite wisdom, provided a practical application of this realization.

During the games, a big tent was set up in the Rubber Bowl in Akron. Many of us went there to pray around the clock. Some of my Christian friends even housed athletes and ministered to them, and we had opportunities to share the gospel message. A man from Amsterdam shared his powerful testimony of how the Lord had transformed his life. He'd been one of the ambassadors for the gay games, but the Lord had seized him. By God's design, he and I spent considerable time together that week. I provided his transportation, so we spent many hours praying and sharing about our lives. God provided him as a covering for me that week. We both went to the opening ceremony at the Q (Quicken Loans Arena) in downtown Cleveland. In hindsight, neither of us deemed that to be a wise choice, but regardless, we were there together. When unknown strangers tried to lay hands on me in a biblical sense, screaming oddities in my ear, he stepped in to provide a strong caution that I was never to allow this unless I was confident in their walk with the Lord and knew them. What a solid word and a built-in protection in that particular moment.

One night, four of us walked almost twelve miles in Cleveland neighborhoods. We prayed and rejoiced, unaware that we were walking through some of the most threatening streets of downtown Cleveland.

Since the gay games, my sincere hope is that something shifted in the heart of the church. I am curious how homosexuality is such a set-apart sin in the church and wonder what would happen in a room full of professing Christians when asked the following questions:

Are you capable of lying?

Are you capable of cheating?

Are you capable of homosexuality?

I suspect the third question might cause a poignant silence. There might be one brave soul lifting their hand, but even that person would look around to see who might join them before thrusting their hand in the air.

Homosexuality has an ingrained stigma. However, the only thing that differentiates any of us is the pure grace of God. As my mother would say, "Given the right circumstances, any of us are capable of any sin under the sun. Only by the grace of God go I." I believe if this was understood, parents would freely solicit the prayers of their friends when their sons or daughters declared "I am gay." The possible pride that takes a hit by not having the ideal family would be immediately squelched by loving friends in the body of Christ. Men and women would be safe to share their struggles in accountability groups without the prospect of "that look," or worse, a shunning because the other person became afraid to engage them further. I sincerely hope this prompts thought. God may want to use you, similar to how He used my dear mentor, to love a struggler into wholeness and stick by him or her for a lifetime.

A Deepened Walk

God has continued to do a deep work in my life through studies of Scripture and a strong net of friends, the majority of whom have not left my side. One study in particular was especially profound because through it I gained a much higher view of God. I stopped seeing heaven and eternity as all about me. Heaven became all about God and the deep worship of Him. Bible reading dramatically altered from a pill-gathering session where I simply seek verses as medicine for the day to real listening and prayer. I have the most freedom of all at this point in my life, but the freedom is constrained by the love of Christ—such an eye-opening experience.

In the LC, I had burned all my possessions. Years later, I replaced some of those items thrown in the fire that day, and they were in my library of stuff. Those possessions caused me to muse on the past, reminding me of people, places, and things that were not edifying. One day, God, through His Word, touched those things and requested I let them go. When He first spoke, I was violently unwilling. Yet each day I would meet Him, and He would speak. I knew it was Him, because His sheep know His voice. Finally, I closed the Bible and said to Him, "I am not willing, so if you want me to do this, you have to work in me the willingness to do it." Philippians 2:13 states, "For it is God who is at work in you both to will and to do His good pleasure."

I sat there for a couple of hours, waiting. I could not stand that the Lord's voice had gone quiet. It felt like rejection and abandonment, and I hated it. Soon the tears flowed, and I could feel Him massaging my heart and birthing willingness. I got rid of those things, and I didn't miss them or have resentment or regret. Why? Because He did it. It was not man's rules inflicted upon me. It was the result of an intimate walk with Him. That day on the beach in the LC, I experienced depravity and depression. Yet on the day I obeyed God's Word and allowed Him to work in me, I rejoiced. Such a glorious contrast about what it meant to truly follow Him.

God had been giving me examples of what it meant to name rightly and hold all things against the standard of the truth of His Word. When Adam was in the garden, God gave Adam the authority to name all the animals. This mission flowed from God down through Adam because Adam was in relationship with God; therefore, whatever he named would be named "rightly." By the same token, David was a shepherd in the field before coming out to the place where Goliath would be challenged. David had been communing with God in that field one to one. When David saw Goliath, he rightly named exactly who he was and had no fear in doing so. In view of these two stories, I realized that the only way we as humans could properly name what was sin and what was in line with the ultimate purposes of God was to be aligned with Him daily in His Word. People can rename to their hearts' desire; however, that will never change God's design, original intent, and *His* naming.

Returning to Your First Love

The Lord had given me a picture of a bride at the back of the aisle. The bridegroom had known his bride from the time she was small. Anticipation by the bridegroom was immense. His eyes danced as he gazed upon the apple of his eye. He knew that he had unlimited love and provision despite paying an enormous price for this day.

As the bride began her journey down the aisle, her eyes were fixed on him. She carried a small bouquet of fresh-cut roses. Then out of the corner of her eye, she was drawn to a massive array of rainbow-colored flowers held by an imposter whose face was hidden. She decided to take a redirect, simply to smell, and was propelled into the narrow pews. The flowers were lifeless yet laced with an intoxicating aroma. As she breathed in the scent, the fragrance anesthetized her, and she barely noticed the horrific face that held the alluring counterfeit bouquet.

Her focus blurred, she lost her footing, and the crowd started to cheer. They tugged at her hair in intrigue and removed all the pins that held it in place. As the mauling continued, she collapsed. Jeers and sneers surrounded her as one by one these uninvited guests took advantage. Their footprints and handprints, resembling soot from a fire, covered her torn and tattered dress. The jewels were all stolen, but her clenched fists barred them from removing her ring.

The bridegroom kept calling her name, but the deafening noise of the crowd dwarfed his still, small voice. He was heartbroken she'd taken her eyes off him, yet he would never force her to love him. The bridegroom witnessed the entire scene. He did not depart, as his heart still longed for his bride. Soon the crowds dispersed, the lights went out, and the bride was unable to move. Her breath was shallow, her heart ached with despair, and she was convinced that she had lost her bridegroom forever. In her destitute and dark state, she cried, "Are you there?"

Immediately he was so close that she felt the very breath of his words impart healing to her lifeless body. She knew his voice. He lifted her to himself and provided a brand-new garment, and she returned to the one she had known for a long time. The crowd had been unsuccessful in removing the ring because they had no power to change the fact that she belonged to him.

This bride was me. I had inhaled the mantra of the world's system and was suffocated by a false impression of love. I betrayed my first love and chased after another. My clothes were tattered and my insides were shredded. But the Lord kept His promise and covenant from the time I was five and a half years old. Although the journey had tragic detours and diabolical choices, He never let go. The scarlet cord tethered, the ring of promise remained, and He would finish what He started.

When I read the Word, I often feel His very breath transforming me, His very hands wiping away tears of pain and heartache, and those same hands cupping my cheeks, resulting in mutual smiles of delight. There are also many times when He is challenging me toward obedience. I try to ignore and cling to some fantasy that I will ultimately win the argument. Yet in His gracious way, He keeps prodding and imparts in me the willingness to surrender, recognizing that His way affords the greatest joy. I am so grateful to be in the Lord's grip. I did not do anything to deserve His healing touch and His provision. He drew me in kindness to repentance.

When I celebrated my sixtieth birthday in 2017, I had to scale the list down to seventy invites, all from Ohio with the exception of a few. The Lord gave me the following speech for that day, representing an appropriate close to this book.

When I look back on this particular decade, it is with tremendous awe and astonishment because nothing about it was common. On the day I turned fifty, I was high up in the Andes Mountains on a mule. There was a three-thousand-foot drop on one side, and the trail was no more than three feet wide. I had to completely trust the mule I was riding to get me safe to my destination. For certain there was nothing I was going to do to aid this animal. The irony was that I trusted the mule to the degree that I actually let go of the reins. With both hands free, I was able to photograph amazing panoramas that the others did not even notice because they had their heads down with a death grip on the reins. They were all jealous of my shots upon our arrival. I had not relinquished the reins of my life to the God who formed and knew me before time, yet I was willing to abandon my safety, security, and longevity to a mule.

That was then. In the summer of 2008, at fifty-one years old, God planted the seed through a job offer of northeast Ohio, a quite unexpected place. Yet through a contemplative eleven-hour plane ride back from the UK, I was actually excited about the prospect. At this juncture in my life, I was riddled with guilt on my poor mothering skills and was not that happy with my life in general. I had been holding the reins of my life, and it had already cost me dearly. So maybe a new landscape would afford peace.

I thought I had decided to move to Ohio, but I must tell you, it was ordered before time, and it set in motion a decade of repentance, forgiveness, relational restoration—especially with my beautiful daughter—peace, and immense joy.

Now let's discuss this house in Ohio. The previous owner designed and built this house. When I moved in, I was intrigued by the wide hallways and doors, the ramps that provided 100 percent accessibility to every area, and even closets with low racks, which being vertically challenged, I noticed. It all seemed quite random until the day I met her disabled granddaughter. I saw that this apparent random plan was far from random. It was deliberate, filled with purpose, and designed with a specific human being in mind. What a picture of how I am to view my life. My Creator had a design and a purpose before time. I simply enter into the realization of it day by day as I get to know the designer in an intimate way and follow His leading.

So as I look back, apparently random meetings of people and the relationships that develop, events that change a course—are anything but random. This decade, in concert with my whole life, has been landscaped perfectly, and all of you, friends and family, represent a million pixels of color and personality that have enlivened, strengthened, encouraged, and incredibly blessed my life. All of you are unique, yet each one of you has a place in my heart that fits just right. He designated before time that I would be in relationship with you.

Many of you have prayed deeply for me, and I can honestly say that at different junctures, I have prayed for each of you by name and certainly thanked God deeply for all of you.

By God's grace, my home has housed nations: India, China, Vietnam, France, and Iran. More rice has been cooked in my kitchen than all of your rice feasts combined, and I bet none of you have ever had one thousand frozen cicadas in your freezer as a daily breakfast delicacy. Yet with all these different cultures, it has taught me flexibility, shown me what is not a big deal, and also revealed how similar we really are if we are willing to make ourselves vulnerable.

Many years ago I read a book, and a small paragraph seized me with a statement declaring that it was a good idea to daily consider one's funeral and what you desire for attendees to comment and remember. It went on to say that by taking such a daily mental time out, this premise will guide your daily life and how you act. I have never forgotten this charge and, immediately upon reading it, put it into daily practice.

Here is what I consider each day:

Do I have any unresolved conflict or unforgiveness? If so, I ask God to grant a speedy change in my own heart and a relational encounter that will repair the breach.

Have I become so "adult" or so old that I can no longer embrace the vulnerability of a child or too complex and cluttered that I miss the wonder? Oh, may that never be. God says come as a child, and I never want to lose that magic, wonder, and hope that ensue when embracing Christ replaces hanging on to past pain.

Do I care too much about appearance to seize the moment and be silly, crazy, or neurotically excited? I hope not. I love to dance like no one is watching, except if Elizabeth is watching, I spare her the agony (at least most of the time).

Is there anything in the way between me and God? If so, I ask Him to grant me the grace, strength, and willpower to release it, stop it, or move in His direction. The most agonizing thing for me is when I cannot hear God speak.

Do I have eyes to see people and ears to listen, not to just the words they say but really hear and attempt to understand and make myself available? Let me be sensitive to catch the moment and resolved to stay put within the framework without looking at the time.

Am I willing to be known—an epistle read and known—unafraid, knowing that my experiences are never just for me? Sometimes a daunting challenge, as hurt might be right around the bend.

Have I let go of the reins of my life today, or am I trying to control it? Do I truly believe that the entirety of the landscape that the Lord designed and ordered will yield the greatest joy and that peace issues from surrender to Christ? This is a daily exercise bolstered by intimacy with the Lord.

I lost much prior to this decade, and much of that loss was self-inflicted: holding so tight to the reins, deciding what was best and what would make me happy, rebelling for my own perceived desire. I watched as the locusts spiritually, psychologically, emotionally, and physically consumed everything. Nothing escaped the ravages. Yet in the last eight and a half years, God has restored all the years the locust ate. Look around. This is the visual of what it looks like—all of you! A field of renewal and restoration. No one is just some haphazard encounter. You have been hand delivered to me by God as a precious and wonderful gift. The oldest relationship, my ex-husband, yet dear friend Peter, a gift. My precious daughter, an incredible gift and shining example of extended forgiveness and love. The collage of faces and memories that will simply continue as a lifetime love gift.

The body of Christ and friends within and without are important to me. I am extroverted, sensitive, and relational. Friends are now in proper perspective. God desires us to have intimate relationships with others, but within the bounds of His design and for His glory.

I will never stop fearlessly sharing the gospel message and being vulnerable with my testimony. I have traveled all over the world, whether for business or pleasure, and have been blessed with many encounters that might only be just once. We scatter the seeds, water, and pray. But ultimately it is God who causes the growth, and we must never forget that it is *His* mission.

This book is my little epistle that I have been called to share. It is *my* story and *my* journey with the Lord. It is not meant to be prescriptive. My prayer is that you have been deeply impacted and encouraged by God's keeping power, His perspective and landscape, His amazing grace, and the power of prayer. If you are a discouraged parent or relative of a loved one, please don't isolate yourself and walk it alone, and don't let pride rob you of experiencing the multifaceted living God. His desire is to embrace you on the journey and open you to the multitude of marchers and prayer warriors willing to stand by your side and stay the course.

I am sensitive to the fact that the mere subject matter will potentially press the nerves of some, inflame, or incite hearty debate. I get that, and you may deem the book suitable for "file thirteen." I won't be offended. However, I simply ask that you keep your trash bin close by. God may want you to retrieve this again someday and open your heart to a bird's-eye view of His love and destiny for *your life* as well. In the meantime, we can lovingly agree to disagree.

Author's Notes

Closing Remarks on the LC

A lthough my experience in the LC was one that I would not want to relive, I would never claim that the LC was a cult. *Cult* has many connotations extending from improprieties with money, sexual garbage, and a whole slew of other things. Suffice it to say it was extreme. It stole my youth to a large degree, yet I occasionally wonder where my youth would have ended up had I not been sheltered in this framework by the sovereign hand of God. Did God condone all that occurred? Of course not, but God saw the whole landscape before I was born. Although the Word was force fed and indigestible much of the time, it was still the Word.

God's Word never returns void. I learned truth, whether palatable or not, and there were many moments where that truth seized my heart and I was excited about it. I can recall many other divine minutes in church meetings where I did experience Christ, and I cannot deny them as trite. They were real. There was a point in a Revelation training that I attended where I almost leaped from my chair as I pondered my eternal destiny. Most importantly, the truth of God's Word kept my conscience active and heightened even when I would make a deadly choice for darkness.

About a year ago, I contacted Vee, the woman I first lived with in the LC. Her son had just died from a rare condition, and I felt compelled to reach out and offer support. That was definitely a prompting by the Lord, because we ended up having a two-hour conversation. I realized that God keeps transforming all of us. Healing and restoration occurred without any rehashing of the past. It was a blessing and another indicator that the Lord cares about the details.

Many who have left the LC have never fully recovered and hold deep resentment and bitterness toward God. I can tell you assuredly that I am not one of those people, and I attribute it to God's amazing grace. I have forgiven what occurred, but it does not change the fact that the ramifications continued for a number of years after my departure. I'm grateful that nothing is wasted in God's kingdom. He uses everything for His purpose, and the LC was no exception.

Saved or Not Saved? That Is the Question

Some of you may be pondering the question right now. How can someone who received Christ at a young age end up in the depths of homosexuality? This is a large debate among Christians. Was I redeemed by the blood of Christ, or was my conscience simply activated? I do not have a good response. I only know my life. In writing this book, it is evident to me that God sees the entire book—beginning to end. We see it chronologically in the space of time, but He sees it as a whole life all at once.

Paul's writing in Philippians 1:6 states, "For I am confident of this very thing, that He who began a good work in you will perfect it until the day of Christ Jesus." I don't see an "if" statement in this sentence. What I see is that He who began will *finish*. God's work in me will not conclude until I die and meet Him in eternity, and it is on His timetable.

Am I Straight?

I must clarify the verses in Luke 3:4–6. People have been in awe that those were the verses I landed on, because they refer to "making straight" as a literal thing. That is not what God did in my life. People sometimes believe that the opposite of homosexuality is heterosexuality. However, the opposite is holiness. I was not magically changed into a full-blown heterosexual ready for men and marriage. Absolutely not. I still notice beautiful women, but I am challenged to live out 2 Corinthians 10:5: "We are taking every thought captive to the obedience of Christ."

I do not consider myself straight or gay. I simply identify as a child of God who strives to surrender to His will on a day-by-day basis. To identify any other way is to mix my relationship with God with a human identity when He calls me to vertically identify with Him and Him alone. He will take care of all the human (horizontal) relationships. I do not try to predict the future. Instead, I savor each day as if it were my last and stand in wonderment and curiosity about what God will do next.

God Is Never Too Late and Never Too Early—He Is Right on Time

Some might say, "Well, thankfully, she finally got to the point of healing." But I cannot dismiss a single element of the journey or the glorious scarlet thread and the places of grace where I was held by the living God. He never left. In the Bible, when Lazarus died, the Lord did not show up right away. The space of days was to ensure that He received all the glory and to increase their faith. The space in my life may have been years in the natural world, but if one day is as a thousand years to the Lord, then in reality the space was just a few minutes!

Remembrance—My Dear Mother

Juanita "Penny" Overstreet
January 26, 1926–April 6, 2018

J ust prior to completion of this book, my dear mother went to be with the Lord. These are my words of remembrance shared at her memorial service.

As I pondered the last couple of weeks what to write, there were a number of perspectives that came to mind. My relationship with my mom was multifaceted with layers of complexity because life and we humans are complicated at best. However, in the end as I was praying, I realized that there is only one perspective that matters when compiling a memorial about a person's life. It is what God saw before she was ever conceived. It is the days He numbered and ordered as she walked with Him, and most of all it is what He said when she finally left this life and entered into a glorious place. When I was able to wholeheartedly embrace and bask in this reality, the true reality of a life well lived, the words came and the tears came because I saw grace and mercy unfold before my eyes like never before. I saw the love of God even deeper than I have known it in my own life for many years. So today, what I speak to you is what truly matters.

As I convey these words, I do not think that my mother is looking down on me or even looking down on this memorial service. Why? Because the glorious one she is viewing this day has captivated her sight—the one she loved since her early thirties, yet never saw face to face, is now in her view, and her eyes are fixed. If there are truly no tears and no sorrow in heaven, then it is contradictory to say that she is looking down at us and all that fills this earthly life. This memorial is for us to remember her and ponder the legacy of a walk with God that will hopefully compel us toward the same and be relentless to find and know the one that she knew for sixty-plus years.

My mother conveyed two key truths to me at a very young age: Never own the offense that another suffers, and let forgiveness be your guide. Recognize that apart from Christ, you are capable of any sin under the sun.

These truths have been markers in my life and still hold. I personally believe my mother saw the depths of her brokenness without Christ. Many say people come to Christ because they have a need and they are too weak in themselves. Thank heavens for such dependence, as my mother knew that we were not meant to live our lives independent from God. So to me, the greatest exhibbition of her strength was dependence on God seasoned with humility. This is contrary to the human way. However, my mother did it God's way. I am confident that each day my mother opened up her Bible daily, repented daily, experienced forgiveness, and gained deep joy. She knew God's promise that the work He started in her, He would finish, and she was humbled by that promise. She did not try to rush God. In fact, even though marriage was not easy, my mom and dad were able to reconcile and forgive many things in their eighties. That is grace, my friends, and that is what God sees.

Holidays in our home were simple. We had a simple tree and just a few small presents. However, I knew the center of Christmas, and that was the focus. Easter, we dressed in our cute clothes. However, I knew it was the most important holiday ever because of the cross and resurrection—that was the focus. My mother did not dress in finery and attempt to look to the "nines" when she exited the home. However, each morning she clothed herself with Christ and His Word, and the Lord saw that clothing. She lived a disciplined and organized life, yet she allowed herself to be so lovingly disciplined by God.

My mother knew that her children were a gift. She never took credit for the good we did, and she also never blamed herself for the bad stuff. Why? Because she knew that we were in God's hands and that her hands were no match for His. However, she prayed. Oh my, did she pray. From the time we were born, she prayed about every aspect of our lives. When I made some choices that grieved her deeply, she was never ashamed of me—it never injured her pride. She loved and she prayed.

Her favorite story in the Bible was the woman at the well. This woman came to a well in the heat of the day all by herself, yet Jesus, while on this earth, purposely came to the same well to meet her. He knew this woman was alone and broken, and He gave her living water that would last for an eternity and satisfy her deepest longing. That woman left behind her empty water pot, as she no longer needed it. The Lord knew every broken aspect and every flaw in this woman's life, yet He saw her, and she was the apple of His eye. When this woman experienced the Lord, she was never the same. My mother drank of this divine living water, and each day this water transformed her life.

Typically, when we ponder a life well lived, we look at the outward things—all the "goodness" that we perceive as good. We have our own litmus test that we have designed and developed based on life experiences and our own definition of goodness. We elevate identities—good parent, good businessperson, charitable, kind, loving, et cetera. Don't get me wrong—these are all very admirable qualities for sure.

However, in the end my mother knew that there was only *one* litmus test that stands when she enters heaven's gates: a relationship with the One who created her—not just knowing about Him but knowing Him in an intimate way and allowing Him to be the center and Lord of her life. When the Lord greeted my mom, I know it was with open arms and a big smile and the words that He said were, "Well done, Penny." He had delivered the letter in His Word, and she had responded back to Him for sixty years. Now they were simply meeting face to face in a glorious reunion—not unknown but known.

In honoring my mother today, I know in the depths of my heart that her desire for all of you is that you get a bird's-eye view into the One she honored, the One she is captivated by right now in heaven. My mother would say to you that this earthly life was never meant to be her best life.

Her goal was not to be happy. Her goal was to allow God to transform her from the inside out. However, in the midst of it all there was deep joy. So for her, the best life is now. All the complexity and hardship of life have been narrowed to a singular and simplistic view. Her identity is Christ and Christ alone, and that is what stands for all eternity. All the rest has been peeled away and turned to dust.

As we emptied the house, I realized the futility of things. In the end they are piled in a heap and taken away. But the Christ in my mother's life could never be taken away. She now gets to experience Him in full, and to be honest, as I wrote this, I am kind of jealous that she gets to dance with Jesus.

I love and honor my dear mom. I choose to cling to the only perspective that matters. I choose to remember an unrelenting walk with God. I choose to remember a mother who prayed and loved unconditionally. I choose to remember a mother who thankfully pointed me to Christ.

I myself know what it means to be an imperfect mom, and I am certain my daughter could underscore this. No one gave us little handbooks at the door of the hospital, but as a parent I have also come to recognize what my own mother grasped at her core—we make mistakes, we love deeply, we cry in despair, but we cling mightily to the rich hope in Christ and trust that He makes all things new. My mother knew that she could *not* know Christ for me. Yet she knew the power of prayer and that prayer changes everything. It certainly changed me, and I am eternally grateful for her constancy and deep love. What a legacy she imparted. I certainly hope that when my own daughter stands at my memorial someday that the legacies I have left behind will mirror those I have conveyed today—the ones that truly matter.

Thank you, Mom, for humbling yourself before the Lord and embracing a Savior. Thank you for introducing me to that same Savior, and thank you for praying me into my own personal walk with Him. I will look forward to seeing you again, and I too crave the words I know you received: "Well done!"

Order Information

REDEMPTION
P R E S S

To order additional copies of this book, please visit
www.redemption-press.com.
Also available on Amazon.com and BarnesandNoble.com
or by calling toll free 1-844-2REDEEM.